Praise for
Human(Kind)

"Ashlee is an elegant and intelligent writer, an eloquent and passionate communicator, and a brave and kind voice in our community. Ashlee teaches by example how to live with courage and compassion, and I believe her perspective and voice will be deeply meaningful to so many people."

—SHAUNA NIEQUIST, *New York Times* best-selling author
of *Present Over Perfect* and *Bread & Wine*

"*Human(Kind)* will change the way you engage with every single person from this point forward. Ashlee Eiland brilliantly uses stories and unpacks Scripture to guide you toward rediscovering the good and upholding the dignity of all. This book is a must-read!"

—STEVE CARTER, pastor and author of *This Invitational Life*

"If we aspire to be kind—to recognize the inherent value in every human—how may our aspirations culminate in our attitudes, actions, and interactions in everyday life? Ashlee so beautifully offers us delicacies that feed this very desire, crafted from her experiences of everyday life that were anything but. This book is a feast she invites us to share, seasoned generously with thoughts to stimulate our understanding of one another, images to awaken our hearts, and wisdom to nourish our souls."

—CAREY AND TONI NIEUWHOF, Connexus Church

"Brené Brown said, 'Courage gives us a voice and compassion gives us an ear.' And in *Human(Kind),* Ashlee teaches us the importance of both. Through her deeply personal stories and thoughtful reflections on the world she currently exists in and the brighter, more just future she is actively cocreating, Ashlee shows us the often messy but worthy way of redemption and reconciliation. I am so grateful for Ashlee as a teacher, sister, and leader."

—LIZ FORKIN BOHANNON, founder of Sseko Designs
and author of *Beginner's Pluck*

"In her tenderly written book, Ashlee draws on a range of personal experiences to explore how life fashions identity. She reflects on big themes, from the love of family to the brutality of racism and the search for belonging, and calls us to greater awareness of the stories and systems still shaping our lives and communities. Through her deeply personal words, Ashlee leads us toward a grace-filled vision of humanity in which we see the *imago Dei* in ourselves and one another and live it in the everyday. 'Human(Kind)' indeed."

—JO SAXTON, leadership coach and author of *The Dream of You*

"Through her beautiful gift of storytelling, Ashlee Eiland compels you to slow down, to breathe and take time, to enter into story after story, to probe into your own story, and, most important, to reflect on what it means to both believe and follow Christ."

—REV. EUGENE CHO, founder of One Day's Wages and author
of *Thou Shalt Not Be a Jerk*

"*Human(Kind)* is proof that God wants to use every part of our wild and precious lives to transform us and influence others. With a knack for storytelling and a passion for kindness, Ashlee authentically and vulnerably invites us to explore the good, the difficult, and the seemingly mundane moments of our lives for God's purposes and the good of humankind."

—MEGAN FATE MARSHMAN, author of *SelfLess* and coauthor
of *7 Family Ministry Essentials*

"In an era of increasing isolation, Ashlee offers a beautiful gift: the opportunity to see the world through her eyes. With vivid storytelling, uncommon wisdom, and breathtaking empathy, she helps us notice daily invitations into a kinder and braver way of being human. Powerful and deeply needed."

—AARON NIEQUIST, author of *The Eternal Current*

"Ashlee Eiland is an incredible teacher and writer. With a distinct voice filled with depth and grace, she inspires and challenges people of all races and backgrounds to take one more step toward humankindness."

—AUSTIN CHANNING BROWN, speaker and best-selling author of *I'm Still Here*

"In her revealing and enthralling debut, . . . [Ashlee Eiland] expounds on themes such as sacrifice, honor, respect, acceptance, gratitude, rejection, commitment, and loss. . . . Readers looking to cultivate more empathy— toward others and toward themselves—will enjoy Eiland's wise testament."

—*Publishers Weekly* starred review

HUMAN
(KIND)

FOREWORD BY DANIELLE STRICKLAND

ASHLEE EILAND

HUMAN (KIND)

HOW RECLAIMING HUMAN WORTH and EMBRACING RADICAL KINDNESS WILL BRING US BACK TOGETHER

WATERBROOK

Human(Kind)

Scripture quotations marked (ESV) are taken from the Holy Bible, English Standard Version, ESV® Text Edition® (2016), copyright © 2001 by Crossway Bibles, a publishing ministry of Good News Publishers. All rights reserved. Scripture quotations marked (MSG) are taken from The Message. Copyright © by Eugene H. Peterson 1993, 1994, 1995, 1996, 2000, 2001, 2002. Used by permission of NavPress. All rights reserved. Represented by Tyndale House Publishers Inc. Scripture quotations marked (NIV) are taken from the Holy Bible, New International Version®, NIV®. Copyright © 1973, 1978, 1984, 2011 by Biblica Inc.® Used by permission. All rights reserved worldwide. Scripture quotations marked (NLT) are taken from the Holy Bible, New Living Translation, copyright © 1996, 2004, 2007, 2013, 2015 by Tyndale House Foundation. Used by permission of Tyndale House Publishers Inc., Carol Stream, Illinois 60188. All rights reserved.

Trade Paperback ISBN 978-0-525-65343-1
eBook ISBN 978-0-525-65344-8

Published in the United States by WaterBrook, an imprint of Random House, a division of Penguin Random House LLC.

WATERBROOK® and its deer colophon are registered trademarks of Penguin Random House LLC.

Library of Congress Cataloging-in-Publication Data
Names: Eiland, Ashlee, author.
Title: Human(kind) : how reclaiming human worth and embracing radical kindness will bring us back together / Ashlee Eiland.
Description: First Edition. | Colorado Springs : WaterBrook, 2020. | Includes bibliographical references.
Identifiers: LCCN 2019025048 | ISBN 9780525653431 (trade paperback) | ISBN 9780525653448 (ebook)
Subjects: LCSH: Kindness—Religious aspects—Christianity. | Christian life.
Classification: LCC BV4647.K5 E35 2020 | DDC 241/.4—dc23
LC record available at https://lccn.loc.gov/2019025048

Printed in the United States of America
2020—First Edition

10 9 8 7 6 5 4 3 2 1

SPECIAL SALES
Most WaterBrook books are available at special quantity discounts when purchased in bulk by corporations, organizations, and special-interest groups. Custom imprinting or excerpting can also be done to fit special needs. For information, please email specialmarketscms@penguin randomhouse.com.

For Delwin, Brooklyn, Myles, and Journey.
You are, without question, the greatest
evidence of God's kindness to me.

We are together in this. Our human compassion binds us the one to the other—not in pity or patronisingly, but as human beings who have learnt how to turn our common suffering into hope for the future.

—Nelson Mandela, December 6, 2000
Johannesburg, South Africa

Contents

Foreword

This world is a mess. Our world is a mess. My world is a mess. Even typing that feels cathartic somehow because it's the truth. Amid the complexity of the messy problems in our world—racism, sexism, and violence, just to name a few—grows fear. That fear manifests in our everyday lives in the way we distance ourselves from one another. We are afraid to engage. We are afraid of conversation; our lives have become full of subjects too sensitive and difficult to bring up. So we stick to weather and sports, clinging to whatever is polite enough to ensure we stay out of the tension. Living this way makes us feel uncertain and overwhelmed and paralyzes our best efforts to connect. Is there a remedy?

In *Human(Kind),* Ashlee Eiland offers us a deep tonic for our condition. Far more than a self-help formula that alleviates any tension, her invitation to try kindness is a terribly beautiful offer. The cynical among us may scoff at the idea that something so simple could be a way out of our current cycles of pain. But simple does not equal easy. This is an invitation to come out from behind the walls of complexity and despair and get to the task in front of us. Even before that, it's an invitation to get to the task *inside* us—to start applying kindness to ourselves.

I'm honored that Ashlee has welcomed me into her life. She has navigated a rich variety of circumstances to find herself here, in a wise and generous place. The word *kind* describes her well. The pain and beauty of her life are infused here with an opportunity to rediscover our own humanity through another lens. As I read these stories, so beautifully crafted and honestly shared, I wonder who Ashlee is. I find myself trying to define her. Is she an African American woman searching for value, belonging, and connection in a world full of racial tension and confusion? The answer is yes. And yet she is more than that. Is she a strong, wide-eyed, curious girl growing into a wise and whole leader in a church filled with sexism? Yes, she is, and yet there is more. Is she a contemplative seeker, yearning for depth in a shallow, functional, success-driven culture? Yes, she is, but there is more. Is she a mother who longs to nurture and lead other little humans into the fullness of God's sacred callings? Yes, she is, but there is more. And that's what kindness does, I suppose. It helps us look into and beyond our typical defining labels. It breaks open the boxes we have put ourselves in. Suddenly, we have the open space to explore what else we are and could be and might even become if we gave ourselves permission to explore the *more* of ourselves and of one another.

Ashlee is not just one thing—she is human and therefore complex. Her situation is unique and common at the same time. She is a holy, mysterious, beautiful creation who has a sacred glow in the deepest part of her, a divine yes right at the center. And discovering this is the core call of this book—to move beyond the categories and limitations we put on one another and even the ones we put on ourselves. To uncover the longings, the divine invitation, the sacred image in one another. To uproot buried hopes and possibilities and nurse them back to life—using kindness as a potent remedy. Resurrection power is found in the simple truth that kindness might just be able to bring us all back to life. So be curious, honest, grateful, and friendly, and don't avoid sacrifice, commitment, rejection, or loss, because if we are kind, these things become portals to healing and wholeness.

—Danielle Strickland, author, speaker,
and social justice advocate

A Rescue Mission

Be kind to one another, tenderhearted, forgiving
one another, as God in Christ forgave you.

—Ephesians 4:32, ESV

Kindness is such a mushy word. When I think of kindness, I automatically picture people who smile a lot, particularly in situations that would easily frustrate the rest of us. When they're cut off in traffic, they smile. They may even *wave* to wish the offender well. Kind people are unfailingly polite and considerate, usually thinking of others first. When someone gives them harsh or critical feedback, they receive it graciously and without defensiveness. Nothing seems to shake their composure or positive outlook. They simply chuckle in the face of mild adversity and go on about their day. If we're honest, most of us find these folks refreshing, yet mildly annoying. If kindness were personified, it'd be one of *those* people: smiley, gentle, potentially passive. They might be respected but aren't necessarily invited to lend their perspective on wildly important matters.

My perception of kindness in its purest form—maybe yours too—is that it's really reserved only for the likes of perfect preschool teachers or professional do-gooders like Mother Teresa and Mister Rogers. We often think kindness has no place in the arena of hard-hitting debate and truth-telling activism. If one chooses to bring kindness along, that person is often considered naive, unsophisticated, or—worse yet—weak. It is not a legitimate contender in the ring of human disagreement.

My first job was as an associate at a Blockbuster video store. I was a part of the esteemed cohort of film connoisseurs responsible for transferring all our VHS tapes to DVDs. But before we made the full transition, the familiar saying remained plastered on our exit door for all patrons to see: Be Kind. Rewind.

We often treat kindness as an afterthought or a suggestion that we shouldn't take seriously.

Be kind. Wash your hands.

Be kind. Recycle.

Be kind. Return your cart.

All nice things to do, surely. But when it comes to the conversations and discussions that matter—the ones wherein we defend our values and ideals, our platforms and politics—we expect kindness to take a back seat.

However, I've become convinced that kindness (and its cousins compassion and empathy) must be rescued. If we let it, kindness will be a part of what saves us from the divisions and disharmony that have become cemented in how we coexist, from the sting when we talk about what grieves us and moves us to action, and from the pride of our postures online and across tables as we advocate for that which we believe in so strongly.

Kindness will be able to undo the damage we've done because it's the secret weapon for detecting the intrinsic worth found in every person.

But in order to see the power of kindness on display, we'll always have to sacrifice something, whether it is time or impatience or the dominance of our own opinions. Transformational kindness toward other humans will also require something that frenzied fingers flying across a keyboard never have: bravery. It takes a brave person to come out of hiding, to come off a Twitter feed or Instagram live video and sit in the flesh with another human being who was crafted with intentionality and great love, injected with the *imago Dei*, the image of God himself.

It takes bravery to look someone in the eye, choosing to believe that person is worthy and choosing to be changed by intentionally engaging both kindly and respectfully with one whom the Creator called "very good" (Genesis 1:31, NIV).

In Ephesians 4 the apostle Paul charged the church at Ephesus to be kind to one another. This was after he called them to maintain unity and right before he urged them to live lives based in love, as Christ did by sacrificing his very life for them. He called them to "get rid of all bitterness, rage and anger, brawling and slander, along with every form of malice" (verse 31, NIV). All these negative traits seem to thrive in our current culture.

In its original Greek the word *chrēstos*, which we translate *kind*, means "useful toward others," "good-natured," and "gentle."[1] Jesus used the same word in the gospel of Luke when he spoke these words to his disciples and the multitude: "Love your enemies! Do good to them. Lend to them without expecting to be repaid. Then your reward from heaven will be very great, and you will truly be acting as children of the Most High, for he is *kind* to those who are unthankful and wicked" (Luke 6:35, NLT, emphasis added).

Loving an enemy? Super hard. I'd argue that it's harder than debating that same enemy on social media or gossiping about him in the break room. But Jesus commanded it because he did it first. He even told us how kind his Father is to people he calls ungrateful and wicked! I'm pretty sure we all have a list of folks we'd consider wicked or who seem at least loosely acquainted with evildoing. Jesus and Paul called us to be actively useful toward them, to be good-natured and gentle. Therefore, I'd argue that extending kindness is a lot harder—and a lot more powerful—than we give it credit for.

Kindness does more than facilitate easy pleasantries or cordiality. It melts swords in the arena. It bargains with clenched fists, inviting those fists to become open hands in the ring. Kindness helps us see beyond mere words to our hearts and shows us, truly, how suffering has shaped us and taught us to treat one another. It gives us hope and catalyzes healing between parents and children, neighbors, and nations.

Kindness may be a mushy word, but it's the dark horse of our humanity. It's not loud or demanding, but given enough time, it wins.

———

If we're going to find our way back to one another—to be bound together once again—we must start with relearning how to be kind to ourselves. By examining our own stories, looking at both our wounds and our most admirable qualities, we can discover when and where we were taught to love or defend or hide. We can find clues to our wholeness and the gaping holes in need of love and appreciation and belonging.

Each of us has a story like this—a story that taught us something about humankindness.

As we explore what has formed us, we can give kindness another go. We can look at the people and places that trigger us. We can absorb the blows to our pride. Maybe we'll even choose to consider a different perspective because kindness has taught us how to be patient with and gracious to the people and stories all around us.

This is my story—a story of a black woman who grew up in the South and who discovered some wholeness and some holes along the way. As I looked back over my life, there were moments I remembered so vividly. Upon further reflection, they were vivid because they mattered. They marked me in both beautiful and painful ways. But as I sat with these moments and memories, I realized they mattered because they taught me how to be kind to my own worthy self. Recalling them helped me acknowledge the good gifts I've been given, the gifts I now hope to give to others, and enabled me to see the painful and hard moments as opportunities to be more fully human, to remind myself to receive grace where there's been grievance. In seeing my story and learning how to be kind to myself, I'm reminded that we all have stories. We all have good gifts and hard grievances. But the sum of both equips us to engage others, even those who are difficult to love, with the kindness we find in Scripture, transforming us into something better and more unified.

Laced throughout the book are invitations for you to revisit the stories of your own life, to understand more fully how you have been formed along the way. Saying yes to these invitations will require openness, courage, and a lot of kindness. But if we are bold and brave, kindness will do its work of elevating our stories and rekindling our common love and humanity. Kindness will bind us together, helping us reclaim our worth once again.

1

Good Hygiene
(Curiosity)

The school I attended from kindergarten through twelfth grade was an excellent one. I'm not just saying that out of personal pride because I attended it or because it was one of the first schools to equip every student with a laptop starting in the seventh grade. I'm also not proclaiming its excellence simply because I attended this all-girls private Catholic school during the hype surrounding Britney Spears's first album release, the cover and the contents of which were every plaid-wearing schoolgirl's shout of legitimacy.

My school was excellent, in my opinion, because of the nuns.

The nuns who lived on the picturesque campus in a white columned home we all called the White House were mostly elderly and kept to themselves—but there were a few in particular who absolutely defined my experience.

One nun wore shin-length skirts that were usually more festive and memorable than those worn by the other sisters. She wore eyeglasses and rocked wild salt-and-pepper hair that never truly fit the *Sister Act*–inspired image of a nun. She was one of my high school English teachers.

Her cultural relevance combined with her caffeine-fueled energy and nontraditional garb made her one of the most beloved teachers who ever walked the hallways of our school.

Another nun who lived in the White House—the matriarch in many respects—was older and more delicate, but what she lacked in physical strength, she made up for in quick wit and stern instructions. She was the glue that held all of us together, as she was present, accessible, and genuine when it came to matters involving our personal lives. Her wisdom and knowledge of our school's history tied our younger generation to her rich roots. Her presence bridged the gap from the good ol' days to the promise of our present.

There were other standouts too—such as my kindergarten teacher, who sat me in timeout for saying "pee-pee" too loudly. (She also made me cry when she told our class that a strange little man had stolen our freshly baked cookies and we had to go on a hunt around the school to get them back. She was referring to the gingerbread man. I was not amused.) Oddly enough, she turned out to be one of my favorite teachers. My experience of her began to shift when she brought out the primary-colored parachute during library time and when she helped us tackle messy papier-mâché projects, like the oversized stegosaurus named Stephanie that we constructed.

Given our proximity to all the nuns, it's no surprise there was much intrigue and curiosity on our quaint little wooded campus about the White House. We all wanted to go inside.

One of the only ways in was by participating in Extended Day, which was an after-school program specifically structured for girls whose parents (or nannies or neighbors) couldn't get to school for pickup by three thirty.

If you were one of the lucky few girls who were hanging around like perfectly good pieces of cantaloupe on a tray of fruit, you walked through the school building, across the campus, and down a long boarded pathway composed of neatly spaced wooden slats—a pair of high heel's worst nightmare—to the fine arts building. There, you checked in with a teacher, dropped your bags, grabbed a snack (usually Goldfish or Cheez-It crackers) that you placed into your perfectly pleated napkin pocket—and you waited.

If your parent didn't arrive by six o'clock, you had the privilege and honor of an exclusive all-access pass through the heavy White House doors. Inside, the nuns would feed you a modest meal for dinner. But most of the time, your parent arrived within that two-and-a-half-hour window and there was nothing to brag about the next day in the hallways by the cubbies.

I entered the White House twice under these circumstances.

On one such afternoon—I must've been six or seven—I made the familiar trek through the school and across campus to the fine arts building. I swung open the glass door and dropped my JanSport backpack, the *thud* echoing all the way to the top of the pointed glass ceiling. I rounded the corner, collected my snack, and began rummaging through the kitchen cabinets to find Mille Bornes, my favorite card game.

As I spread my snack and the cards on the faded green Victorian rug, a little girl plopped down in front of me. She had sand-colored skin and soft brown hair that was pulled back in a long ponytail, safely secured by a navy-blue ribbon. Her plaid jumper matched mine. Her white socks hosted a fringe of lace. I noted that I hadn't met her before.

"Can I play with you?" she asked softly.

"Sure," I said, without much thought.

"I don't know how to play," she confessed.

"It's okay," I said, crunching my Goldfish. "I'll teach you."

As I dealt her hand, I glanced up periodically to catch her blue eyes. She was staring at my arm. At around seven years old, I didn't know exactly what was coming next—but I knew I was under her microscope. Self-conscious, I rubbed my right thumb over a patch of sand that had hung on for dear life after my afternoon tour around the sandbox.

"Do you shower?" she finally asked me, her head cocked to the side.

"What do you mean?" I asked, crunching more Goldfish.

"Your skin . . . ," she began. Then she stopped. "I mean, your skin looks really dirty. Does your mommy help you shower every day?"

I felt a sudden sting in the lower pockets of my eyelids. I knew tears were close, but I didn't want to make a scene in front of this curious stranger.

"Of course," I choked out as I attempted to appear controlled and even. "Of course I shower. I mean, I usually bathe in a bathtub."

"Then why does your skin look like that?"

"Because I'm African American and I have dark skin."

Her mouth twitched to the side as she stared at my arm without any regard to my discomfort.

We didn't play Mille Bornes that afternoon, and I didn't finish my Goldfish. I abandoned the carpet and raced to my backpack, tore it open, and pretended to read a book.

My mother eventually picked me up, well before the magic deadline. I could smell the scent of her perfume and hard work on her clothes—and I told her everything. Empathetic—and, I know now, silently seething over the ways she couldn't protect me—she listened and assured me that I wasn't dirty and that I was beautiful.

My mother and father worked long hours, climbed their way to the tops of their fields in the Texas oil and chemical industries, and made sure our lives were comfortable. They made sure I could attend this excellent school and dream the same dreams of exclusive access and behind-the-scenes privilege as the sixty-two out of sixty-six girls in my class who weren't black.

I was lucky to be the beneficiary of their hard work.

But that one afternoon taught me how curiosity shapes and forms us. Sometimes we become nosy, jealous, or envious of another's experience. At other times, we long to draw close and know more, genuinely wanting to be charitable, kind, and helpful in relationship. On one side of curiosity, we're the explorer, searching for answers and hoping to know more about why or how someone else exists. But on the receiving end, curiosity can do the opposite work. It can make us feel like a specimen being poked at on the biology table, like a betta fish in a really small bowl. We're not invited into anything. Rather, we're examined and then left alone. Curiosity can be a catalyst for real relationship, or it can isolate and exotify, making someone feel completely "other."

I don't think the little girl who sat before me that day was malicious or ill willed. I think in her childlike curiosity, she wanted to tell the truth; she wanted to be friends and to know more. She genuinely wanted to help me.

But sometimes even the most innocent, childlike curiosity doesn't lead to great discoveries. Instead, it can inadvertently lead to years of confusion and even more questions that require a delicate undoing—an undoing that some of us are still trying to navigate with careful intentionality. For me, that undoing has been slow, deliberate, and thoughtful—an everyday and yet mostly invisible part of my existence.

I spent years trying to convince myself that I wasn't dirty, that I was worthy to walk the hallways of my excellent school with the standout nuns and to take up space. I spent years trying to remind myself that I was one of the lucky few. But sometimes, I learned, being lucky and having opportunities make you stand out in all the wrong ways.

I realized that gazing at the inside of the White House wasn't as glamorous as we all made it out to be. Gazing, digging deeper for the sake of more information, doesn't always pay dividends in the context of real relationship. Our curiosity may be satiated, but at what cost? Sometimes the cost is a glaring dent or a hole filled with even more questions. As far as the White House was concerned, if you got the answers you wanted—if you were one of the last ones left—giddy curiosity met harsh reality. The reality meant you stood outside the front door in the dark, waiting for someone to answer.

2

Cherie

(Sacrifice)

There's something subtly remarkable in recalling the people your parents chose to care for you when they were away. The people who protected you and looked after your well-being in their absence were critically important. While I was at school, it was the nuns and Extended Day teachers. When my parents went on dates or needed to go to parties and work functions, more often than not I went to Cherie's house.

Our family lived about twenty-five minutes from Cherie, which felt like an eternity back then. It was a straight shot down one farm-to-market road, but there were countless stoplights hindering us from getting there quickly. Go, slow down, stop. Go, slow down, stop. For twenty-five minutes. Looking back, I'm sure my parents could've figured out other, more convenient childcare options, but there was only one Cherie. My mother recalls seeing a man and a woman on a walk one evening while driving through another neighborhood. They were holding hands and strolling along as if they had nothing but time to be with each other. She remembers thinking how loving they seemed. Little did she know, that was Cherie, walking hand in hand with her husband. One thing led to another, and through a mutual friend, my mother became acquainted with Cherie. The rest was history. Over the years we grew so close to her family that I don't remember ever ringing their doorbell or entering their one-story brick house through the front door. I couldn't even tell you what color the front door was if you asked me.

My parents always parked on Cherie's short, slanted cement driveway, and we walked through the garage and the back door into the laundry room. During the short journey, we were quite likely to encounter at least one of the eight cats—sometimes the dog. Inside, the washer and dryer greeted us, and oftentimes there was a cat perched atop a rumbling machine, soothed by the massage. Then there was frequently another cat curled up for a nap on the counter in the kitchen. From there, through the living room and dining room and bedrooms, each door revealed another creature: two birds, a couple of ferrets named after old-school Houston Rockets legends Mario Elie and Sam Cassell, a tank full of fish, a snake—and a tub filled with mice that I quickly learned weren't just for show.

But my parents trusted Cherie. And for good reason. She'd successfully raised four kids of her own and had earned a reputation for being a responsible and nurturing caregiver. Since my parents played club volleyball and had friends in that neighborhood, they heard about her quite a bit. As I got to know her myself, I came to love her humble spirit and quick smile, her eager and willing attentiveness, and her hospitality.

I don't remember ever seeing Cherie with shoes on her feet. Her spirit was like her wispy blond hair: free and light. Yet the lines on her face hinted at the triumph and trial of motherhood: raising two gorgeous, strong-willed daughters and two hardworking sons, plus caring for her grandkids, who I pretended were my little brothers and sisters. She smelled like the smoke from her cigarettes, but the scent was sweet, and it grew to be familiar and even comforting to me.

No one ever mentioned the fact that Cherie and her family were white—and that my family and I were black. No one ever had to. When

I was under her roof, I felt as if I were her priority. I felt that she enjoyed having me there. I had access to the fullness of her life; she wasn't hiding anything from me. I felt as if I were another one of her kids, receiving the best of her. Black or not, I felt I belonged.

Cherie's house was a major backdrop of my early life and so much a part of me it felt like a second home. It was an oasis made of brick and mortar, a retreat where I was invited to adventure and explore, a new strand of freedom tucking itself into the folds of my fragile identity each time I visited. I remember going barefoot in the backyard, tiptoeing across the pavement's pebbles, and sinking my feet into the cold, damp grass.

I didn't know many black kids who were allowed to go outside barefoot. At least, I don't remember it being encouraged in our house. Perhaps my parents wanted my feet to be protected from any scratches or scrapes or anthills. After all, our ancestors had spent too many years trying to preserve the dignity of their own brown feet: bare feet that were often shackled and enchained. Covered feet were better. They were safe.

But at Cherie's, my shoes came off—and I was free. I was the free little black girl stitched into the fabric of Cherie's white family, privy not just to her pets but to all the drama too: forbidden tattoos and job dilemmas and arguments and breakups. I was the unassuming yet ever-present little black sister.

———

As free as I felt in Cherie's care, there was one time when it became clear that her care, unlike her love, had limitations.

One day, my mother dropped me off at Cherie's and had a conversation with her about my hair. I imagine it went something like this:

"Hey, Cherie," my mom said. "Thanks again for taking Ashlee. I really appreciate it, especially on such short notice. I don't know what kind of fun you have up your sleeves for today, but if her hair gets wet, don't worry about washing it."

"Are you sure?" Cherie asked in response.

"I'm sure," my mom said.

Then my mother would've left, confident and happy knowing her daughter was confident and happy in this white woman's home. I'm sure she suspected we'd be playing in the sand or splashing around in the water from the hose out front and I would soon need to be cleaned up or dried off.

But she also knew that Cherie, as much as she loved me, had no idea how to care for my head of black-girl hair. Cherie knew how to nurture my wit and adventurous spirit; she knew how to meet my needs for food and sleep. She knew how to bring my creativity to life as we played dress-up and watched the fish swim in her tank. She knew so much about how to care for me.

But my hair? She had no clue.

I don't remember what we did that day, but I do know that when my mother came to pick me up, my thick, kinky hair was in knots. A comb was stuck in the strands, my curly black tresses were knotted between porcelain-white fingers—and Cherie was in tears.

"Cherie! Are you okay? Why'd you wash it? I told you not to worry about washing it."

More tears.

I don't know why Cherie was crying. Maybe she was frustrated because the shampoo that cleansed and moisturized and smoothed her hair wasn't having the same effect on mine. Perhaps she felt frustrated with herself because instead of heeding my mother's words, she had taken them more as a suggestion. Perhaps she was anxious about how my mother would react to seeing her daughter that way.

I wonder if more than anything, Cherie felt a sense of deep shame. Shame that her actions had caused more harm than good. Shame that she couldn't care for me in this way just as she'd shown her care for me by making me sauerkraut for dinner, letting me taste coffee with too much sugar for the first time, or giving me a kitten of my own for my sixth birthday. Maybe Cherie felt shame because she, as a white woman, had no idea how to care for such an important part of my being—my hair.

Out of charity and true love, Cherie had attempted to tackle something she knew nothing about. And what I imagine she ran into was a shocking realization that as much as she knew how to love me—how to help me kick off my shoes and run freely into new adventures that would shape my sense of freedom and belonging—she would never know what it meant to manage my blackness.

I'll never know for sure how Cherie felt about that day. But although I felt as if I belonged in her family, I later realized there would be some aspects of my identity that she would never be able to shape, form, or tease out with the capable fine-tooth combs of her smile and her warmth. She taught me humility, grace, authenticity, and the joy and comfort that can be found in simple things—in, say, a bowl of sauerkraut and a cup of coffee. She taught me what it means to welcome strangers and treat them like family—to set them free and encourage their sense of discovery and delight in little, everyday things.

But Cherie couldn't teach me, a young black girl with thick black hair, to love my blackness. She could tell me it belonged, but she couldn't tell me how to embrace and defend it for myself.

She couldn't teach me how to see my blackness for what it really was outside the safe haven of her home. She couldn't teach me to care for it when it would surely be battered from stares and name calling and discriminatory work practices. She couldn't teach me to make it my own, giving it its own unique expression, a runway for its fullness.

Cherie gave me so much, but she couldn't give me that.

Cherie passed away when I was in college. Even after I'd graduated from high school, I'd call her on her landline—a number I still have etched in my memory to this day—so we could catch up. After she got sick and as her illness progressed, I talked more and she talked less. Then her daughters would relay my side of the conversation to Cherie and talk for her. Eventually, there was only silence on the other end.

Today, I silently honor this woman every time I walk around my home with bare feet or drink a cup of oversugared coffee. I honor her and her family's legacy in my life whenever I walk into someone's home and see more than one cat lounging around or sauerkraut offered on a sandwich board. I honor her when I visit the zoo with my kids and answer their million questions about animals, holding close the memory of Cherie's own little zoo.

I honor her for what she gave me—and for the ways she tried so hard to give me what she never could.

To me, sacrifice means giving up something important or valued for the sake of others. Cherie wasn't perfect. But she sacrificed, regularly. She embodied sacrifice in the way she gave up her valued space: her comfy couches and her warm pebbled porch. She gave up her very body: her strong embraces and her wide smiles whenever I came inside with a scraped knee or elbow. She gave up her ramen and coffee and tablespoons of sugar—even one of her kittens—all for my sake.

At their best, our loved ones often try as hard as they can to give us everything we need. They sacrifice for us, trying to give us freedom and permission to be our best selves and to live unencumbered. They give up their finances and dreams so we can pursue the dreams birthed from our own childlike awe and wonder.

But real love for another human can take a different form, one that says, *The pressure's off, and I still accept your love.* Because despite the willingness of others to sacrifice, there are aspects of you and me that are galaxies away from their ability to understand, parts that are completely unknown or too complex to explain. If someone else were to hold these parts of our identities between their fingers, they'd be too puzzling to figure out, like a Rubik's Cube with ten of one color, when there should be only nine.

So, we have a choice. Either we can resent the fact that some people can't give us everything and demand that they try harder, that they sacrifice even more of themselves. Or we can sit patiently under the comb, knowing in our hearts that the outcome might be less than desirable—but also knowing that trying is the best offering some can give.

When I left Cherie's house that day, my hair was in knots, but my heart was intact. And to this day, I can confidently say that I imagine my dreams and desires with such freedom because of what Cherie *did* give me all those years ago.

For all her trying and all her sacrifice, I honor her.

3

Alaska

(Honor)

I never thought black people lived in Alaska. It's not that I didn't believe black people *could* live in Alaska—I just never thought any black person would want to. All I knew about Alaska was that it was far away—and cold. My ancestors did hot. We traced my dad's DNA back to the Balanta tribe in Guinea-Bissau. We traced my mother's bloodline to Liberia. My people did coastal heat and warm water. Not glacier caps.

But then my godparents and godbrother moved to Anchorage, and my family and I suddenly had an excuse to go visit three black people who lived there. I don't remember the entirety of that trip, but I can see it in snapshots, like slightly overexposed Polaroids spread out on a worn and rustic table.

As much as I was wrestling with what it meant to be a black girl in America, even before I was conscious of it, there was a moment in Alaska that revealed something good about who I was. Something that stuck.

The good stuff rarely sticks.

So often, I've defined myself by the hard stuff in my life. I'm guessing most of us do that. We identify with the abandonments and the letdowns, the times we've fallen short or screwed up. We let the hard and cold terrain of life events hack away at us, like a visionless artist might attack a block of ice. But I know there's good to be found in all of us. It was formed somewhere, somehow.

A small sliver of my good was formed in a cold and faraway place, in the least likely of places, to be sure.

In the first Polaroid I remember from the summer of 1992, I'm trying to put a piece of a glacier into a coffee mug, my young mind willing to defy physical science as I hoped against hope I could save it for my friends back home to see. I remember the souvenir shirt my godparents bought for me, which read "Sportfish of Alaska" and had nine different fish that are native to the region, all in cartoon form. (One fish's name was Sockeye Sammy. He looked as if he'd had the hardest start in life with his black eye and boxing gloves.) I remember our car got stuck in traffic on a one-way road. From the back seat, I thought it was because of rush hour or an accident. But when I leaned my thick pigtails with their brightly colored plastic barrettes against the window, I saw a moose. The moose was refusing to cross the street. She towered over the cars, her antlers wide and regal, as if to say, *You're not going anywhere. None of you. Not until I say so.* And we didn't. We didn't go anywhere until a park ranger came and somehow coaxed her and her calf off the concrete and back into their world.

One day during our visit, my parents took my godbrother and me to the Anchorage Museum of History and Art, where a handful of the 3,600 or so black veterans who helped build the Alaskan section of the Alaska Highway were being honored. The Alaska Highway, completed in October of 1942 after a little more than eight months of grueling work, helped defend Alaska from attack by Japan during World War II. The 1,500-mile road was built by more than 10,000 soldiers—but the black soldiers were segregated in their own units. The project has been cited as "not only the greatest engineering feat of the Second World War," but also "a triumph over racism."[2] The military became the first agency in America to integrate, in large part because of the black soldiers' dedication and hard work during the highway's construction, even when they were poorly clothed and fed meager portions of food.

Of course, I didn't understand the ceremony's significance when I was five years old. All I saw were black soldiers lined up at the front of a banquet room, all sharply dressed in suits and ornate hats decorated with pins and patches marking their years of sacrifice. The ceremony was underwhelming, and time passed slowly—aided by the scratchy patterned conference chairs and the institutional fluorescent lighting.

But it was the first time I remember seeing black men—and only black men—being honored, on purpose. *How unusual,* I thought, *that I had to come all the way to Alaska to see this.*

It wasn't unusual to witness honor being given. I'd seen PBS specials honoring important people. I'd been to prize ceremonies at school. What was unusual was seeing honor being given exclusively to someone who looked like me. Where were the white men? Where were the Asian and Latino men? Why just black men? I know now what I didn't know then: black men are rarely honored on purpose. And if they are, their honor comes late—and rarely by anyone other than other black men or women. It took years for the black veterans of the Alaska Highway to be recognized.

There seems to be room for honor when it is deemed socially acceptable or even personally beneficial to do so. We like to honor those who make us proud—people who are wealthy, brave, well known, successful by our own standards—or those we personally look up to as our muses and our heroes. I don't know many majority-culture people who naturally think of obscure men and women of color as their heroes. If their names aren't Martin Luther King Jr. or Rosa Parks, are they really anybody *that* important? What seemed true back then still seems true today: if one is fighting for equality, that person is probably also fighting for honor. So many people are still fighting for both in this country.

So, despite the scratchy seating and the harsh lighting, the ceremony was a big deal.

When the ceremony ended, I grabbed my father's hand as we made our way out the door and into the cold. It was sunny, but the wind was sharp, lifting our jackets and scooching us along the sidewalk as if it were hurrying us out of the elements and into the car. But before we could round the corner, I looked to my left and saw him.

You know a moment is important when it seems to happen in slow motion.

The man's skin was dark brown and leathery, like a well-loved pair of work boots. The wrinkles in his arms folded one over the other, sagging from old age and what I guessed had been a difficult life. Sitting cross-legged on the concrete in a tattered white T-shirt, he said nothing as we passed, but he did something so unexpected that it caught me off guard.

He looked me in the eye.

When he looked up from his folded hands, his eyes met mine. There was something so gentle about them, soft even. In a split second, I could sense he was holding resolve and acceptance along with raw truth and hardship. He smiled, said nothing, and looked back down.

Sitting next to him was a little white plastic cup, like one you get from Chili's with a kid's meal—too flimsy to keep, yet too sturdy to mindlessly throw away.

I yanked my hand out of my father's grasp and stopped walking. "Dad?" I asked. "Do you have any change in your pocket?"

My father, without asking any questions or interrupting the conversation he'd started with my mother, paused long enough to reach into his pockets and pull out a handful of change.

"Here you go, darling," he said. No questions, no hesitation.

I pivoted on the sidewalk and headed with purpose back toward the man. No one stopped me to ask where I was going. In just a few paces, my skinny brown legs were squarely in front of him, his eyes meeting mine again in a comforting gaze. I felt like I knew him, as if he could have been my favorite uncle or my grandpa who snuck me peppermints when my parents weren't looking. I said nothing for what felt like minutes, though only a few seconds must've ticked by. He continued to smile contentedly without showing any teeth, making neither greeting nor demand, seemingly enjoying my presence.

The change was growing warm in my little hand. I bent down and released the money into his plastic cup, hearing the hollow clash of my coins that signaled they were alone. I stood back up and looked at him again.

"Thank you," he said in a shaky voice.

I smiled. "You're welcome."

I ran back to my dad's side. The adults had waited for me, though they'd been talking the entire time, unaware of the exchange between this man and me.

I took my dad's hand, and we moved toward the car. He continued his conversation. I continued thinking about the man with the tattered shirt and the plastic cup.

Like the ceremony, my change in his cup seemed underwhelming. There were no scratchy seats or fluorescent lights, only a brick wall and some eager wind. But honor was exchanged, held in the space between me and a stranger, dancing in gusts of wind and settling on contented smiles. With few words, he saw me—and he let me see him.

My assumption is that he was homeless. I tell myself a lot of stories about him nowadays: that he'd lost a job, that he was sick and unable to pay his bills, that he was a veteran too.

In a cold and faraway place—a very unlikely place—good was formed in me. In seconds I learned what it meant to see and be seen, even without knowing the whole story. I learned that even when I can't control the outcome or someone else's circumstances, giving honor is still worth it. Standing in front of someone I don't know and affirming his existence can be just as powerful as a formal ceremony. In fact, affirming another individual's existence is even more crucial now than it was when I was five.

There are cold and faraway places all around us—the neighborhoods we won't enter, the family members we refuse to visit, the news channels and Twitter feeds that are off-limits—all based on our personal values and belief systems.

But these people and places have the most potential to teach us. In spite of our discomfort, in the face of the unfamiliar, in the absence of words or answers, we have an opportunity to affirm the truth that both great deeds and great distress can hold room for great humanity. We can see and be seen. We can give and receive. Even without words, we can relearn how to be with one another.

By willingly entering cold and faraway places, we declare with our presence that, yes, good is here. Not just my good deeds or sacrifice. But yours too. The good in you that comes with your life, no matter your story, no matter the hard times you found or that found their way to you.

You are worth a kind and well-meaning stranger's time and genuine smile. We all are. And in declaring so, we assert that the good of our lives is also worthy of honor.

The good that stuck with me from the age of five until now, learned from a man in a tattered shirt, is that good can be found in anyone, anywhere, if only I will stop long enough and honor it.

I learned that in a really cold and faraway place. I learned that in Alaska.

4

Mexia

(Safety)

The most sacred space of my childhood was in a small town whose name I'm still not completely confident pronouncing. Mexia, Texas, a small town with a population of approximately 7,400, is off the beaten path of the beaten path. If you're speeding west down Highway 84 toward Waco, you most definitely might miss it. But in the event that your attention is held for more than four minutes, the highlights of the town are Jim's Krispy Fried Chicken, Sonic Drive-In, a little restaurant called the Drillin' Rig, and, of course, Walmart.

But for me, the best part of Mexia was approaching the driveway of my grandmother's little house. Whenever we passed the sign for Jacks Creek, I knew I could exhale. Right beyond the sign was the brick ranch-style home with the red roof that was so close to the 18-wheelers and cattle trailers passing along the highway that in the still of night, you could hear the zoom of tires and the hum of horns in the master bedroom. The only other sound that was as prominent inside the house was a cuckoo clock that ticked incessantly in the long hallway leading from the cluster of three bedrooms to the main living area. The sound of the clock and the buzz of traffic became so familiar that they blended in with the sound of the sliding door as my grandmother, her Doberman, or I passed in and out of her sprawling backyard.

The act of turning left from the highway onto my grandmother's driveway sent a visceral message to my body: *You can stop fighting now. You're safe here.*

What would I have been fighting, exactly? Sometimes I was fighting against the ever-present and internal dialogue that accompanies the reality of being a girl in grade school. Sometimes I was fighting apathy; other times I was fighting myself—beating myself up for a lower grade than I wanted or a dead end in the process of trying to figure out who my *actual* friends were. I realize now that 18-wheelers and cattle trailers didn't just exist as country props, zooming up and down black highway pavement, extras in the opening scene to my favorite movie. They were symbols of the persistent thoughts and worries and questions racing back and forth between my head and my heart, kicking up dust and noise and insecurity, occasionally running over rare and innocent creatures like confidence and whimsy.

The anticipation of returning to this place saved me more times than I can count.

Safe and sacred spaces are often occupied by safe and sacred people. My grandmother was both.

———

Mema was my mother's mother. She grew up right outside Mexia in a small three-room house on a piece of farmland that still belongs to our family. She was one of fifteen kids and helped her family take care of the produce and animals that served as the family's livelihood. She was smart enough to go to college and get her master's degree, becoming a well-known and respected teacher in the Mexia community.

She married my mom's dad, Luther, who died when my mom was thirteen. Their relationship always puzzled me, mostly because I've seen only one picture of my grandfather and don't know much about him. But also because of the way Mema talked about him. In the stories she told, he always seemed so quiet and accommodating. She was the grit and the guts. Maybe he was actually the strongest man in the world for marrying a woman like her *because* she was strong.

When Mema and my grandfather started dating, he would take her out dancing, and they'd spend late nights smoking and catching up with friends from the area. One time, though, Luther clearly outdid himself. It was a rainy evening, and he'd driven her home after their time out on the town and then parked his car in front of her house. And just like in the old black-and-white movies, they'd begun a round of postdate small talk. I imagine it like this: He was telling her that he'd had a wonderful time. She was reciprocating her enjoyment, careful not to be too enthusiastic, cautious in giving her heart away.

Then, all of a sudden and without warning, Luther fell asleep.

Midsentence, Mema glanced his way and saw Luther hunched over and leaning against the window, the light from a street lamp shining bright enough through the downpour that she could see the outline of his eyelids through the dark shadows of the car, only a small slit of the whites of his eyes visible underneath the brim of his hat.

She sat there, stunned. Seething, really. Because, of course, to fall asleep during a conversation with her meant she wasn't worth his attention or energy. It was raining, and now she'd have to let herself out of the car and walk herself to the front door.

With Luther snoring beside her, Mema took matters into her own hands. She gripped the window crank beside her and rolled her window down midway. Then she leaned over her slumbering lump of a date and did the same to his window. She threw her handbag over her head to try to protect her hair as she unlocked the car, and then she darted to her front door and let herself inside.

Early the next morning, she heard a loud and urgent knock. I can imagine Mema nonchalantly making her way to the door, fully expecting who the visitor might be.

She opened the door and, sure enough, there was Luther—drenched head to toe from the rain.

"Why'd you do that, Eddie Lee?" he exclaimed. (By this point in the story, Mema was always struggling through laughter. She was so proud of herself.)

"Luther," she told him, "if you can't take care of yourself, you sure enough can't take care of me!"

Mic drop.

No words after that. She knew she was right. And he knew she was right too.

A story like this is exactly why she was a safe place for me and others who would enter her home. She always seemed to know she was valuable. Her sense of self-worth and security made her seem so fearless—at least to me. Nothing seemed to rattle her or knock her off her firm two feet. Because of that, she was available to receive with open arms the weary and worn fighters, the insecure and lonely wanderers.

Luther went on to ask Mema to marry him. I wear the ring he gave her on my right ring finger. I can imagine that her sense of dignity was one of the most attractive things about her. She knew what she expected from a partner and how she deserved to be treated. She had no problem reminding Luther or anyone else of that fact.

After Luther died, Mema married Eldridge, a Methodist preacher who built the brick ranch house himself and then died when my mom was in college. Mema lived in that ranch house for over forty years by herself. I'm sure both Luther and Eldridge respected her and loved her well. She wouldn't have agreed to spend her life with either one of them if they hadn't.

Most times when I accompanied her to our family's farm to help her feed our cattle, she'd pull the car over when we turned onto the winding dirt road that led from the highway to the farm and she'd tell me to get out. She'd scoot along the velvety silver bench seat to the passenger side of her old Oldsmobile and wait for me to get in the driver's seat. She'd buckle up and tell me to drive. As an eleven-year-old. Hands gripping the wheel, I drove over the rocks and dirt and tree branches, windows down, breathing in air that smelled of hay and freshly cut grass. When a truck approached, I'd pull over to the side, taking a minute to notice the field of cattle to my right or left. We rarely saw another human in the fifteen minutes it took to travel from her house to the rusty red farm gate.

At the same time, she was teaching me how to demand dignity by gripping the wheel of my own story and taking matters into my own hands. Why wait to learn something at sixteen when I could learn it then? Why spend any more time being afraid or insecure when I could learn how to navigate new and unpaved roads head-on? Driving Mema down a dirt road, windows rolled down, I knew I was safe. Mema knew I was safe. She was teaching me fearlessness in the face of the unknown, to brave dusty roads with confidence and dignity. Confidence and dignity could then follow me to school and into my friendships. They could help me navigate heated arguments and bad dates. They could follow me into my marriage and my parenting. They could follow me because she had shown me how to live it out. She'd gone first.

The weeks I spent at Mema's became a template of sorts. I now realize that the time I spent with a woman who mastered her aloneness and lived a full, rich, meaningful life is what has saved me a million times since my adventures driving with her to the farm.

What seemed like the most uneventful times of my life transformed into the most life-giving space I never hoped for. In the silence of the country, I found room. By learning how to be alone, I learned to love myself. Driving slow and steady on dusty country roads taught me that navigating rough terrain requires self-respect, care, and anticipation.

———

In one of the last years of my grandmother's life, my mother got a call from her. Mema was calling from her kitchen to inform my mother that she'd just run herself over with her truck. *Run herself over. With her truck.* After getting home from the grocery store, Mema had put the truck in park and was unloading bags, but in reaching over the seat, she hit the gear shift. The truck, being on an incline, started rolling backward right as she was walking behind the vehicle to get to the garage door. She fell, and the truck's back wheel ran over both of her legs.

But despite the fact that she was in her nineties, she got up and went inside. She finished putting away her groceries and didn't bother calling 911. A few hours later, she called my mother. We were all freaking out—as most would. But she wasn't. And she was fine.

I think years of demanding dignity for herself made her that strong. No one was telling her she couldn't rebound and get back up, whether from a truck-related accident or any other setback. No one was telling her to doubt herself. She didn't have ads and commercials assaulting her with messages telling her she was weak and needed to change, as the only program I ever saw her watch was the local ten o'clock news on a dinky television with a less-than-reliable antenna. She was simply steady in loving her church, her family's land, and her tiny town the best way she knew how: with her confidence and dignity, her open heart and presence.

Mema died in 2016, a loss that still feels fresh as I sift through cards she wrote me for Christmas and birthdays. I can still hear her voice as I read:

Enclosed you will find twenty dollars, enough I hope to help you to keep looking good. The picture was very photogenic. I'm proud to be the grandmother of such an attractive child.

Confidence and dignity everywhere.

Even though she's gone—and even though her brick ranch house no longer exists as I remember it—something lasting remains.

Mema taught me in the silence and stillness of the country that I could find expansion: An expanded canvas on which I can rediscover myself and even love myself again, perhaps for the millionth time. An expanded perspective through which I can talk myself off ledges and replace harsh messages with truth. An expanded capacity to lovingly welcome both my neighbors and complete strangers who want my space and time—because since I no longer threaten myself, they don't threaten me either.

We all need a safe place where we can explore what lies beyond our brokenness and limitations. Even if that place is available for only moments at a time or is in the middle of nowhere. If it's truly a safe place, it's sacred because it also points us to the safe people who love us well. These are the people who remind us that dignity is ours for the taking, who call us back to our true selves. They're the people who call us out and up, who can catch us when we have nothing left and lift us when we're ready to be strong again.

Find the safe places and, more times than not, you'll find the safe people too. In safety you'll find your feet and your freedom. Perhaps you'll even discover enough of yourself to be a safe place for someone else.

5

The South Side

(Humility)

The South Side, the South Side, everybody do the
South Side, the South Side, yeah.

—Lil Keke, "Southside"

Let me tell you: I *loved* blasting hip-hop from my Volkswagen in high
school. With the windows rolled down and my elbow perched on the
window ledge, I wanted to make sure everyone driving by knew I was, you
know, black. And not just black. But *really* black. Like "I listen to hip-hop
and know all the words because this is my culture and I'm obviously in
touch" black.

Perhaps you, too, are a rap fan and have heard of Lil Keke. Lil Keke's
real name is Marcus Edwards, and he's one of the rappers who makes up
the Screwed Up Click.[3] The S.U.C., as it's otherwise known, is a group
of Houston-based rappers that changed the way rap as an art form was
produced and consumed. DJ Screw, the pioneer of the S.U.C. and the
creative genius behind the "chopped and screwed" movement of the 1990s,
took rap music, slowed it down, and "cut" it up, making songs sound like a

molasses-type of remix that Houstonians, Texans, and other underground rap fans around the nation grew to love.[4]

I was one of those fans. There was only one problem. As much as I loved hip-hop, I didn't grow up on the south side of Houston, the area from which many of these respected Houston rappers and hip-hop artists hailed. I didn't have ties to Third Ward or Missouri City. I couldn't even point out South Park, the area where DJ Screw lived and produced his music, on a Houston-area map.

In high school I was the black girl who drove a brand-new Colorado Red Passat with customized floor mats stitched with golden thread that spelled out "Class of 2005." This car shuttled me between my private school and the upper-middle-class neighborhood where I grew up.

On the northwest side.

I lived on the wrong side of town to be able to actually identify with Lil Keke's and DJ Screw's lyrics. I was, most certainly, *not* riding dirty.[5] It was as if a chasm appeared every time I turned on 97.9 FM—the local hip-hop station—or put a rap album in my CD player. I learned the choruses pretty easily, but there was an irreconcilable disconnect between me and the lyrics to these songs. I bobbed my head up and down in appreciation of the bass lines that shook and rattled my windows. But I held tightly to a secret that rattled me just as forcefully.

As a black girl, I was supposed to be able to resonate with those lyrics. I was supposed to be able to identify with life on another side of town. I was supposed to have all the insider knowledge and be able to translate to my nonblack friends at my Catholic all-girls school what exactly those artists were saying. I was supposed to know the verses seamlessly and effortlessly. But the words never rolled off my tongue as easily as I wanted them to. My secret was that, in reality, I had no clue about the life these artists were expressing with their words. I was peeking through a small carved-out hole in that fence, gazing at someone else's turf. I was trespassing. Yet I so badly wanted to belong to and understand a part of my culture that held so much meaning to so many other people—people who looked like me.

So as I drove from the northwest side of town to my school on the affluent west side, I tripped over verses and stuck with the choruses, nodding my head up and down as if willing myself to say yes in wholehearted agreement to both the swagger and the struggles that Lil Keke and the S.U.C. poetically and passionately detailed. But my yes hit the fence of my actual existence every time, and I realized I would never be able to truly know or understand the words I so badly wanted to own for myself. I kept peeking through the hole, hoping to one day feel like I could cross to the other side unnoticed.

The one legitimate connection I had to the South Side was through my Amateur Athletic Union (AAU) track and field club called the Houston Sonics. I started practicing with the Sonics when I was nine years old. I remember showing up for the first time to the track at Klein High School—right down the street from my house—with butterflies in my stomach. To my pleasant surprise, though, most of the other kids on the track were black. (There was one white girl named Shannon, and she fit right in.) Here I was, finally, in a space where I could breathe just a little bit easier, because on the outside, I belonged.

But that feeling of belonging quickly grew more complicated when I started attending track practices on Thursday nights at Stafford High School—a school located on the south side of town. Usually my mom picked me up from school and drove me the thirty minutes to practice at Stafford. I often spent that time mentally rehearsing how I would enter into a conversation or respond to the girls' inside jokes. The girls there were already friends. They knew all the lyrics to the songs on 97.9 and the dances that went along with them. So I needed the time in the car to psych myself up: to transform from peeping through the fence hole, gazing longingly at my friends' seemingly effortless grasp of our culture, to a straddle stance, ready to leap over.

There was a pretty beat-up railroad track that we had to cross to get to the track field, and every time our black Expedition hit the jagged wooden beams, I pictured myself sprinting for the fence and reaching for the edge of the post, feet hitting the wood. I imagined lifting myself up and over as I rehearsed a hip-hop chorus or shrugged my shoulders to a new beat. I pictured myself landing on the other side with a hard *thud*, and there I was. Time to prove myself.

After my mother stopped the car in the parking lot, I'd change into my practice clothes in the third-row seat and throw open the door. For a while, I assumed my presence came across as relaxed and natural. No more separation between me and the experiences I'd accessed through the car speakers throughout the years. No one seemed to notice how hard a time I was having dealing with the tension of entering a different context as we passed the relay baton back and forth. I would offer delayed laughs, even when I didn't get a joke. I'd smile and clap my hands to the beat on the outer circle when some of my teammates stopped for a dance break between sprints. I pretended to like a boy who liked me, just to be a part of the conversation.

But eventually, I was exposed.

At a track meet one Saturday, I remember lining up under a picnic tent set up in the middle of a field, waiting with three of my teammates to run the 4x400-meter relay. As we were stretching and putting on our track cleats, one of the girls turned to me and asked a question that buried itself so deep that I still turn it over to this day: "Ashlee, why do you talk so 'white'?"

There was a pause that probably lasted only two seconds, but it felt as if DJ Screw had taken the question, slowed it down, and chopped it up. In slow motion I heard the playback, but then—I couldn't talk. I opened my mouth to speak but was so aware of my "white" voice that I reconsidered talking altogether.

Eventually, I managed to choke my way through a short response. "I dunno. I just do."

That was the whole conversation. I don't think this black girl, my teammate, meant to shame me. I think she was genuinely curious as to why her vernacular and mine didn't align, why my words sounded more like Shannon's and not hers. She wanted to figure me out, to understand why I didn't roll my *r*'s or elongate my words like she did.

Perhaps in hearing my response, she figured I was just as curious about it as she was. Was I a fluke? Did something happen? Whatever the reason, after that day I was sure that my talking "white" was the reason I had such a hard time identifying with hip-hop culture. It wasn't that I didn't have access; I did. It wasn't that I wasn't welcomed; I was. It wasn't that I couldn't look the part; I looked like everyone else. But because of the way I talked, I felt tainted—like a bowl of clear water forever changed by a single drop of food dye.

I ended up running with the Sonics for close to nine years, making it to regional, state, and national meets, collecting medals and fond memories along the way. But I also came away with a huge wedge of hyperawareness that divided my South Side friends and me. Just as I longed for the rap and hip-hop lyrics to roll off my tongue, I longed to be familiar with the details of my friends' lives. I wanted to know more than just the chorus, the part that anyone could repeat enough times to sound like a fan. The way I talked, for whatever reason, felt like a barrier to that familiarity.

This question about how I spoke prompted other questions I'd later ask myself, such as *Am I black enough? Do I belong here? Which group of people is mine?* We all have questions and doubts, don't we? They can transform what's rich and sure and clear about our identities into pauses and stutters and caution.

———

I now understand that the way words form off one's tongue do not exclusively win admittance to one cultural group or another. I'm black. I'm *really* black. I understand that my blackness is valid and that I can still find belonging in the folds of others' experiences and truth, as long as I'm invited there. I understand that I'm no better than my South Side friends—and that Shannon is no better than me.

Today, I nod my head up and down when I hear rap and hip-hop music. I confidently sing the choruses and let the verses wash over me—leaning in and listening to an experience that was never mine, trying to appreciate the pain and triumph and rebellion and hustle because deep down I know the artist knows something very powerful that I never will.

I have learned to own my voice. It's not a "white" voice. It's my voice, the voice of a black woman who's been loved and taught and challenged and formed by her mother and father and their mothers and fathers before them. My voice speaks of legacy and history. Of that, I'm sure.

I'm getting better at seeing my own life as worthy and valuable, even when stark differences are called into the open. But in being reminded of those truths, there's also great opportunity to close my mouth, to listen, and to receive. The same opportunity awaits anyone who's ever tried to bridge a chasm of difference or unfamiliarity. It's difficult to do, isn't it? Especially when we're trying so hard to affirm that we belong and that we're enough and that we have people. But when we gladly succumb to the reverent weight of another's life, story, and reality, it's an opportunity to be led by that person, to suspend questions about ourselves, and to make room for lives that aren't our own. It's an opportunity to admit that we can't simply proclaim for ourselves another's acceptance. The point isn't to try to relate to all people and demand they affirm us. It's to proclaim "worthy" over and over again, whether or not others are willing to give us their art, their space . . . or even their friendship.

My cultural experience and identity are legitimate. They're not diminished by another's experience or identity. Those things that feel different—such as Lil Keke's lyrics—are now an opportunity to receive, to hold an experience that's not mine but that is just as real and worthy and valuable.

As we peek through holes in fences as eager observers, we can feel steady in what's ours to hold. We don't have to feel threatened or ashamed. Whether the choruses and verses are familiar or completely outside our experiences, it may be in the intersection of the two where humility is found.

6

Camping While Black

(Adventure)

B lack people don't camp. At least, that's the general consensus. It's not even a stereotype, really. It's just a fact. I've never met black people who camp on a regular basis. I'm sure there are plenty of us who like camping and are maybe even camping right now. But, much like croquet or pickle ball or race-car driving, camping does not come to mind when I think of the black experience.

But I've been camping. More than one time.

Let's clear something up. When I say camping, I'm not talking about being away *at* camp, where one stays in cabins or heated lodges equipped with full-size beds, refrigerators, toilets, and showers. I'm also not talking about parking *on* a campsite in a fully furnished RV where you can sleep inside, separated from nature by a physical door with a handle and comforted by cool air flowing from a built-in AC unit. Just to clarify, this is called "glamping."

I'm talking tents. Campfires. Going potty in the woods. Catching fish with your bare hands and eating them for breakfast, lunch, and dinner. This is the type of camping I was subjected to by my mom, dad, and their band of camping compadres.

My parents' circle of friends is the kind of community some people wish for their whole lives but never find. When I was growing up, there were consistently about three to five couples my parents did life with for Valentine's Day, Christmas, and New Year's Eve. If there was a holiday to celebrate, there was a party to throw. The adults got dressed up and went out, spouses often in coordinating outfits, to someone's home or to a hotel or restaurant, ready to serenade a significant other for karaoke night or dance and eat in celebration of yet another milestone of friendship.

These celebratory habits were generally accepted and encouraged by me and the other party "orphans." We ended up forming a little community of self-sufficient preteens and teenagers, huddling in my godbrother's room or somewhere on the other end of the party site, figuring out ways to entertain ourselves while the grown-ups had their fun.

Then one weekend my parents told me we were going camping. I was so confused. *We don't camp,* I thought. And by "we" I meant black people.

But before I knew it, we'd loaded up our sheltie, some tents and coolers, and bags filled with camping gear and attire. All brand-new. We then set our sights on Bastrop, Texas—a little town on the outskirts of Austin that was about a two-hour drive from our house in Houston.

There was at least one perk from the outset: to make trips more enjoyable for me as an only child, my parents often encouraged me to invite a friend from school to keep me company. This trip was no different. My friend Brittany accompanied me, and we met a boy named Cedric at the campsite, a family friend of one of the other couples. Add Cedric's friend and another couple's son, and there we were: five black city kids and a dog, silently staring at one another across a campfire, shiny camping chair tags waving in the smoke-stained wind. The adults picked up where they left off, laughing and telling stories, smooth jazz and R & B providing a soundtrack for the rustic scenery. But we kids were not laughing.

After all, we were camping. Far from the comforts of our Nintendos and *SimCity,* we were out of our element—and yet we were forced to give this camping thing a try.

To keep ourselves busy, the five of us kids eventually figured out that we could play cards and volleyball. Brittany and I took the dog on walks to the water, doing a weird preteen girl thing where we avoided the boys at all costs one minute and then tried to convince them to hang out with us the next. It was so much emotional work. Far from leisurely.

Then there was the work of trying to keep my hairdo intact. I wrapped my thick black hair in my satin bandanna at night, just as I was accustomed to doing at home. But because I didn't wash my hair every day (this is part of the magic of certain types of black-girl hair, in case you didn't know), my hair would absorb the smell of campfire smoke, my silky and perm-straightened strands battling the stench of burnt s'mores and slightly overdone hot dogs.

Here I was, out of my element once again. This time, in the middle of nowhere.

My family did this camping trip to Bastrop at least a handful of times, and each time the same scene was set: at least a couple of black city kids saturating themselves with layer upon layer of mosquito spray, playing some sort of sport or dealing cards around a campfire, listening in on the adults' stories and outbursts of laughter. That was camping.

On one such trip, the weather forecaster was predicting intense rain and thunderstorms during our stay. We took our chances, being familiar with the unpredictability of Texas weather. The forecast could call for clear and sunny and, somehow, you'd wind up drenched, or the meteorologist could send you to the grocery to stock up on water, canned goods, and masking tape, predicting the apocalypse, and . . . ta-da! Beach day.

When we got to the campsite, there wasn't a cloud in the sky. We unpacked our bags, set up our tents, and got the fire going. Cedric was there—avoiding me, most likely. I remember digging through my backpack, trying to decide whether I was going to take a walk by myself or actually do some of my math homework. One family was setting up a brand-new RV—which completely broke our camping rules, mind you. But it was a welcome addition. No one wanted to admit that we envied its AC and shade, which provided shelter from the heavy flannel blanket that is central Texas heat and humidity.

Sitting near the campfire with my math book, I could hear my dad and his friend cracking jokes. My mom was getting a meal ready with her girlfriend when we heard it: muffled shouting. The sound pierced the still air, went silent for a few seconds—and then we heard it again. I looked up, and in the distance, coming up the dusty hill to our campsite, was my Uncle Lonnie—huffing as his short frame race-walked toward our stuff, moving with a sense of urgency. We couldn't hear him, so we all stayed still, holding our books and beverages, waiting for him to get a little bit closer. *Maybe he spotted a black bear,* I thought. Maybe the one toilet at the campsite was clogged. Surely, it wasn't anything too pressing.

Just then, the sky above me went from light powder blue to an ominous puce green. With the snap of a finger, the clouds opened up and water started falling from the sky in sharp sheets. This was more than rain. The wind picked up. The fire was snuffed instantly. The overhang of the new RV blew back, and my dad and his friends lunged instinctively to catch it. Nothing was safe.

As my mom and her friends scrambled to save our things, all I heard was my dad yelling for me and the dog to get in the car. Without another thought, I grabbed our dog and shoved my backpack into our SUV. My shaky hands slipped on the seat belt as I scrambled to fasten myself in. The rear door flew open, and I watched from my seat as the adults stuffed soaking-wet tents, clothes, coolers, and blankets into the back without stopping to determine what belonged to whom. In the midst of the chaos, I looked outside and saw that it was green and clear and still. It was the most eerie mental snapshot of my life. Then it hit me: This wasn't just a storm. It was a tornado.

My parents darted into the car, and my dad revved the engine without a seat belt on. Somehow, he got us out of the campsite and onto the main road without a scratch. As we drove away from the tornado and back toward home, I took note of the musty smell of mold beginning to set in. Everything was wet and muddy. Huddled next to the dog, I was shivering, even though the car's heat was on. My hair was destroyed: only a damp and frizzy crown of curly, shocked strands remained. No satin bandanna could've saved it. Up front, my parents were mostly quiet for the entire two-hour drive.

Finally, back at home, I reached into my bag. My orange math book was twice its original size, the pages and cardboard cover expanded from the water damage. This meant two things: I couldn't do my homework, and all of a sudden, I had a killer story to tell at school on Monday.

We never went camping again.

My parents continued to meet up with their friends for parties and celebrations. I went on to attend my fair share of camps, where, huddled in the safety of a cabin or the luxury of a hotel room, I could wrap my black-girl hair and do my homework in peace, safe from the threat of tornadoes and the anxiety of awkward interactions with introverted boys.

———

Although my camping days are over, I now know what's possible. Before that first declaration that we were, in fact, going camping, I'd made an assumption about what was possible—about what I could and couldn't, should and shouldn't do—based on what I'd seen.

In the absence of an example, I'd drawn a hard line about what could be included in the breadth of my experience, hesitating to participate because "That's just not what we do."

However, choosing to do the things "we just don't do" can lead to some of life's greatest adventures. By diving into experiences, conversations, and relationships we otherwise would never touch, we get to create new memories and potentially confront unintended stereotypes—for our own sake and to rewrite the stories others may try to tell about us.

As the other kids and I grew up and went our separate ways, my parents and the other adults stayed connected and kept up their holiday party traditions. They even met my friends and me in Las Vegas years later as a part of my twenty-first birthday celebration.

Camping was something I didn't love, but I love that we tried it. I love that it helped me connect with nature in a way I'd never experienced before, a connection that is still meaningful to me even now. I love that it allowed me to make friends I never would have met otherwise. I love that I witnessed my parents in relationship with people who mean a lot to them around a campfire and under an RV canopy.

In the end, I love that the thing "we just don't do" became a great story—one that formed new possibilities in my life. That's the genius of adventure, isn't it? It gives us more than just a tale of a singular experience. It also unlocks what *could be*—what *could* become part of our stories. The things we used to be closed off to, the boundaries we used to place around our lives or the lives of other people, are now an open road without a railing, an unobstructed path to expanding what we've previously known to be true. How have we been limiting ourselves? Better yet, how have we been limiting the possibility of what's true in others? Whatever great things we think certain people don't do—I guarantee one of them does. If we're lucky enough to meet or form relationships with people who defy the limiting stories and stereotypes that have been told and held about them, maybe we'll be less surprised when we hear about the mom who has six kids *and* works a full-time job, the eighty-nine-year-old man who still lifts weights at the gym every day, the Latino boy who's really into anime, the high school girl who loves football and made the team—or the black girl who went camping.

Maybe we'll be more empowering, kind, and generous when we think of what's possible in others' communities, cultures, and lives—or even our own. We'll talk about all the places adventure has taken us and what we've learned and how we succeeded along the way, stitching possibility back into the tapestries of our stories. We'll talk about the Bastrop camping trips and the bad storms, the barriers broken and the limits defied. And maybe, one day, people won't be so surprised.

7

Nicknames

(Respect)

I didn't find out until after college that my mom needed fertility treatments to get pregnant. She wasn't old when she had me, by any stretch. She was only thirty-two. Nevertheless, my birth was a result of a lot of intentional thought, prayer, and pain.

I'd heard growing up that I was a miracle baby. Honestly, I thought my parents were just being nice or trying to boost my confidence since I am an only child. But after consecutive years of explicitly telling Santa (in written form, per his request) that all I wanted for Christmas was a baby brother, I realized it wasn't his fault. It wasn't anyone's fault.

At one point, I distinctly remember asking my mom why she and Dad didn't have more kids. "It's not that we didn't want more kids," she said. "God chose to give us you—and that was it."

It's not surprising, then, that the choosing of my name was also painstakingly purposeful.

Lee is a family name. My dad's mother's name was Leola. And Mema's name was Eddie Lee. As my mom's belly grew bigger, both my parents agreed that their child's name would include Lee somewhere, somehow. Then, on a Wednesday in April, my mother didn't show up for work. Her secretary thought it was an April Fools' Day joke. Instead, while everyone else was working, my mom was laboring her precious baby into the world. The surprise of my mom's life was revealed when my dad told her, "You got your girl." Mom burst into tears, resting her head on her hospital pillow, relieved that the exhaustion of childbirth was over and that she had a healthy child. But a decision had to be made.

My parents ended up picking what was the second most popular girls' name in the state the year I was born: Ashley. (The decade should be obvious to you by now.)

But the name Lee still needed to make an appearance. Easy fix. My parents replaced the "ley" in Ashley with "lee." Then my proud, sweet daddy claimed the "sh" in Ashlee as his own, those being his initials. And, ladies and gentlemen, that's how I became A "Sid Holmes" Lee, or Ashlee: the most thoughtfully crafted, second most common, hard-to-explain little girls' name in Texas.

Miracles can be really hard to explain to other people.

Growing up, I got used to hearing people call me Ash. My mother's friend from the Baptist church we attended called me Pooh. (She still calls me that to this day, and it takes me right back to the administration office of the church, which smelled musky and featured 1980s crimson-colored carpet, a couple of office phones, and piles of copy paper. I have no idea what those ladies did with all the paper.)

My parents had plenty of cute nicknames for me such as baby, sugar, and sweetheart.

But it wasn't until I got to high school that *the nicknames*—the ones that would cling like ornaments of cement hanging from my identity— started finding their way to me. These names, birthed in locker-lined hall-ways or crafted in the cafeteria's hot lunch queue, were almost always followed by a burst of laughter. Sometimes that laughter came from my very own throat. What else are you to do when the inventor of a wounding name is your friend? When the originator is your teammate, the upper-classman you look up to, your lab partner? When you actually love the name giver—and absolutely hate the name? Ashlee and Ash weren't enough for some. There was painstaking purpose in these names too. Not all were malicious, but they all subtly communicated what someone else thought about me.

              —

PITA. This name, an abbreviation for the phrase "pain in the _____," was the name given to me by some of the upperclassmen on our varsity basketball team. I was the only freshman who made the varsity team that year. As part of my "welcome package," some felt I needed a name that would keep me in my place—one that would remind me that although I was the only freshman good enough to make it past tryouts, I was still only a freshman. I wasn't great at basketball, but I was good enough. And our team was actually pretty awful that year. But it was the first time I learned that even just a little bit of goodness—goodness that can help you stand out as unique, goodness that comes through hard work and focus and is a source of personal pride and confidence—can and oftentimes will be used against you. Mostly by those who think they have the power to turn someone else's goodness into a straitjacket. People like leaders. People like decision makers. People like varsity team captains.

              —

OJ. One afternoon I was sitting cross-legged in our gym lobby before basketball practice, doing homework with teammates. In between leaning over to talk with someone else about the answer to a homework question and cracking up at our seniors' jokes, I was taking sips of orange juice from a plastic bottle of Ocean Spray. One of the upperclassmen said something unexpectedly hilarious, and I couldn't help it: I laughed midswallow, spraying juice out of my nose and onto another human—and there you have it. Some names are affectionate and benign, harmless enough to be memorable but not traumatizing.

———

Cracker. Then there was this nickname, which is an offensive name for a poor white person. Here's the problem with this one: I wouldn't consider myself thin. The slender frame I had in my younger years became a distant memory when I started playing sports. Obviously, I'm not white. But I didn't fit the stereotype some of my classmates had about how a black girl should talk or act. I was one of just a few black girls in my class, yet I talked and lived more like the white girls did. I knew the same Top 40 songs they sang. I wore the same Doc Martens and swung the same trendy L.L.Bean backpack over my shoulder. I didn't live close, but my house was nice. To them, I was an anomaly. They couldn't figure me out. It was as if I couldn't exist as me, by myself, on my own, different from them, yet sitting at the same tables and taking the same tests. So they gave me the name Cracker. Confession: I remember calling a couple of girls in my class the same thing. I'm not sure why. Maybe I sensed the irony in the fact that I wasn't white and they actually were. It was a subtle way for me to push back—to not feel so powerless—even though I knew it was wrong. They always laughed. I sometimes did. I never liked to.

———

A.Ho. I was in the lunch line at school, talking to an older student about Jennifer Lopez's new album, *J.Lo.* Suddenly, she said, "You know, if you did the same thing with your name [Ashlee + my maiden name, Holmes], you'd be A.Ho." Cue laughter. And not just from one student but from other girls in the lunch line. The name got around—and it didn't leave. Despite the fact that I never had a boyfriend for longer than a few months in high school. Despite the fact that I was pretty naive and straitlaced. My friends knew how reserved I was, but the name was just too good *not* to use. Even after college, friends from high school would text me, still including "A.Ho" somewhere in the message.

As a high schooler, how do you tell other people what not to call you while still preserving relationship? How do you stand up for yourself while also inviting people in, giving them space to love you and be loved within personal boundaries of respect and decency? I didn't know how to do any of that back then. And, honestly, I didn't want to. I wanted to be liked and known as someone who had thick skin. I saw these girls almost every day—some of them for thirteen years straight. My skin was thick, but this name hurt.

It's easier as an adult. You become more selective in choosing who to share space with. But I still grimace when I read those three letters, strung together in such an order, separated only by one defining dot. Those letters didn't reflect any part of my truth; they didn't open the door wide for my identity to freely step forth in confidence. Rather, like toilet paper on a shoe, they followed me, a nuisance, attracting unwanted attention. I wish I could've plucked them off myself as easily as toilet paper.

———

Oreo. This was the most hurtful nickname in my past. We're not talking cookies here. We're talking about a word that's still frequently used in referencing black people who are, as I was told, "Black on the outside, white on the inside." I couldn't argue with the name. My skin was dark, yet I was surrounded by whiteness. Therefore, I mistakenly concluded, the essence of who I was as a person was white. As cookies, Oreos are delicious. I love it when they soften a little bit after being submerged in a glass of milk. In fact, that's how I felt. I felt as if I were being held under, drowned, surrounded by a color that wasn't me at all. I could've fought the name. But sometimes it takes more energy to fight than it does to give in and take the blows—to display your strength by not showing any emotion or concern at all. That's what I did with Oreo.

———

In an appearance on *Oprah's Master Class: The Podcast,* the late poet and author Maya Angelou said, "Words are things. You must be careful, careful about calling people out of their names, using racial pejoratives and sexual pejoratives and all that ignorance. Don't do that. Someday we'll be able to measure the power of words. I think they are things. I think they get on the walls. They get in your wallpaper. They get in your rugs, in your upholstery, and your clothes, and finally, into you."[6]

Names are the most powerful of all the words. They have been carefully chosen, painstakingly picked for us by our parents who wanted to honor their faith, family members, or a favorite icon. Some names are picked because of the way they sound, how they roll off the tongue and nestle themselves into the ears of strangers, potential employers, and lovers.

I'm ashamed to say that I have called people out of their names. I've undermined the care with which they were chosen and missed the honor of mirroring back to people their value. People have certainly called me out of mine. And the names outside my true identity as a deeply loved and cherished daughter of the Most High have, as Maya says, gotten into me.

Growing up, I believed names were personal yet relatively unimportant. Now I know differently. I know I have the power to own or reject a name. I know I have the power to uplift or wound with one. I personally know the impact names can have on the fragile process of claiming one's being, both stepping into and living out of it.

My name is Ashlee. I'm my father's daughter. I'm A "Sid Holmes" Lee. And I'm a miracle baby. My parents intentionally prayed for me and named me with purpose.

But I'm not the only one with purpose. What would it be like to live in a world where the value of who you are, the way you reflect God's image, the meaningful purpose for which you were created was affirmed and called forth before any hurtful names and labels had time to take root? The names that have stained your identity like red wine on white carpet, like dirt caught deep in new, luxurious upholstery. They're the ones you've been thinking about this entire time: Stupid, Four Eyes, Pudgy, Worthless. These names threaten the truth.

That truth is this: no matter what destructive and damaging names you've been called, they aren't the ones that matter. The ones that matter are Worthy, Valuable, Chosen, and Beloved. These names remind you that you weren't, in fact, a mistake but a person who needed to live. They remind you that you would be missed if you were gone, that the pain of rejection won't always sting so badly. They remind you that there's life after loss and that you're not someone's afterthought. You know these names matter because, upon hearing them, you hold your head a little higher. You walk in confidence. You find yourself giving others the same respect given to you because you know how it feels to walk in the truth of who you really are.

Let's do the work of living out of our good, true names and using good, true names of one another. Let's call one another Warrior, Survivor, Teacher, Friend, Artist, Advocate, Hero, and Optimist. The world needs more of what's good and true in us. It needs to be reminded that we're miracles.

8

Blue Shadow
(Choice)

As much as I struggled with my various nicknames, I at least had the gift of adaptability. I'm not even sure where I got it. It was just there at my disposal, ready to use in situations I needed to survive throughout high school, manifesting in tools such as fake smiles, forced laughs, a quick dance move, or an exaggerated eye roll. My adaptability was a catchall, kind of like a fanny pack for my social life.

If I needed to blend in as we were getting ready for Friday night football at the all-boys school, I sang along to Tim McGraw and Brad Paisley. (I still have the *one* country CD that my friend Jackie made for me years ago. I memorized every song, including "Friends in Low Places" by Garth Brooks and "It's Five O'Clock Somewhere" by Alan Jackson and Jimmy Buffett. That CD still comes in handy today. Black girl with a curly Afro belting out country choruses? I've surprised the pants off some people.)

If I needed to liven up a dance floor at homecoming or prom, I could choose from a variety of moves, including "La Macarena," "Cha Cha Slide," or "Cotton Eye Joe."

I learned to roll my plaid skirt at the waist, making it just short enough that I wouldn't look like a nerd but long enough that I wouldn't get caught by one of the nuns and get detention.

My backpack hung by its straps at their longest possible length, the main compartment sagging below my uniform, helping me fit in with the trendier crowd at school. (My mother hated this fad. She swore I was going to get backaches and aggravate my scoliosis. I received an embroidered roller bag at my high school graduation party from one of her friends, which I promptly hid in the back of my parents' coat closet. It's still there, fifteen years later.)

Then there was the world of hair and makeup. The blessing of attending an all-girls Catholic school was that any effort to apply makeup or do hair before school was absolutely unnecessary. It most definitely wasn't needed to impress anyone. Other than the few nuns and teachers roaming the halls (no more than about five of those teachers being men), it was just us girls, 250 or so high school students with the ability to focus on friendship, field hockey, and French.

There was a downside, though. The downside was that I didn't know how to keep a beauty regimen. And I grew to care very little about needing one. It was a huge deal for us girls to start shaving our legs in fifth grade and then eventually to spend every year of high school anticipating no-shave November, when a few girls in our grade competed to see whose leg hair was the longest by the holidays. But outside that, there was no need to worry too much about missing a day of shaving or stubble noticeably poking out from your knee-highs.

The same went for hair and makeup. As a freshman, I never wore makeup to school. My face was always a raw, blank canvas of saggy late-night-study eyes and skin that was constantly fighting acne. (I'm sure I aggravated it by letting sweat stay put too long after basketball and track practices.) I usually wore my hair in a ponytail or messy bun. On *really* special occasions, I wore it straight. There was absolutely no point in spending that much effort on what I felt was trivial, meaningless outward vanity.

Until a certain point.

━━━

Around my sophomore year, when most girls started getting their driver's permits and licenses, a whole new world of social possibility opened up to us. Suddenly, we could drive *ourselves* to football games. We could drive *ourselves* to practices and meets after school. But the most exciting of those possibilities was being able to take ourselves to house parties, hangouts, and after-school functions. Now it wasn't just about the ride over. All of a sudden, there was a point. The point . . . was boys. We needed to fix our faces and "get ready" so we could face the boys.

My getting-ready routine was usually quick and very simple: I penciled on a basic eyeliner that I seemed to *always* end up jabbing in my eye (the residual redness making it look as if I were perpetually suffering from allergies) and swiped on some lip gloss. That was it. No mascara (my eyelashes are already naturally long and thick), no foundation (I could never find the right color to match my dark skin, especially not in the drugstores surrounding my school—because, you know, no demand for black-girl product), no eyebrow pencils or lip liner, and no eye shadow.

I often finished my makeup with enough time to play DJ in my friend's bedroom, swiveling the radio knob from Top 40 to country; put some curls in a friend's hair with her new CHI iron; grab a makeup bag here or a ribbon there. I slid under the radar frequently without anyone demanding more of my routine. I liked it that way. It felt right to me.

Then one day I found myself in the back of a friend's car, headed to a party close to my house. I remember it being bright outside, sunny and clear—a typical spring day in Houston. Gazing out the back-seat window,

I remember zoning out for a split second while two of the girls teased the third about some scraggly boy from another private school who was showing interest, unsuccessfully. It was clear that he was not a welcome suitor, given the fake gagging noises I heard from the front seat.

But my reverie was broken by an unexpected and enthusiastic idea from one of the girls: "Ashlee, you should try some eye shadow! I've never seen you wear any before."

By this time, the car had halted in front of the party house. The two girls in front were now swiveled around, staring at me expectantly. My friend sitting opposite me in the back seat had one hand on her makeup bag, the other on her seat belt, just waiting for my go-ahead.

"I don't think I want any for tonight. My eyes get irritated pretty easily," I responded. I thought about turning and poking myself in the eye to produce some sympathy-inducing redness.

"But it'll make your eyes pop, especially with the shirt you're wearing."

I was wearing her shirt, a ruched, tight, and sleeveless teal number with a low-cut V-neck that the girls had recommended. I felt like a pillow stuffed into a shrunken pillowcase: slightly suffocated but just cozy enough to get the job done without drawing too much unwanted attention. My arms were showing, which, as an athlete, I hated. I was already so aware that they were more muscular than the average sophomore's. And teal was definitely not my color. By that point in high school, I was past the paisley and floral prints stage. I wasn't into color if it wasn't black, gray, navy, olive, or white. Occasionally, I'd wear red or light blue. But teal was just too much for me.

I thought about my friend's request while the two girls in the front seats kept staring. Feeling surrounded, I let out a defeated sigh and muttered, "Sure, why not?"

Squealing, my back-seat buddy unbuckled herself and immediately started rummaging through her makeup kit. Finally, she slowed as she found the palette she was looking for.

For me, everything started happening in slo-mo. Her porcelain-white hand came out of the black bag holding a square compact. She popped the lid, and a wide grin spread across her face. I was terrified.

Now in real time, I looked down at the spread of colors, all shades of blue.

"Close your eyes," she whispered with glee.

I forced my eyes shut and felt the softness of an oval eye shadow brush dance in small strokes across one eyelid. In between the short pauses, I would start to open my eyes, but a "Not yet!" would interrupt my desperation to be done.

Back and forth, the brush danced as it finished one eyelid and skipped over the bridge of my nose to the other, stroke after stroke producing wave after wave of dread.

"Okay! All done!" I heard the palette snap shut as I opened my eyes.

"It looks so good, Ashlee! Here, take a look."

Reluctantly, I leaned forward as my two friends in the front made room. Resting my knee on the center console, I positioned my face squarely in front of the rearview mirror to see what had just happened.

I froze in place, horrified. Bozo. I looked like Bozo the Clown.

Bright blue eye shadow was spread wildly across my eyelids, meeting the bottom of my eyebrows on each side. My throat tightened and tears filled my eyes, holding in position, waiting for my permission to flow.

"Thanks," I said, looking away quickly. I threw open the car door and stood up into the fresh air, inhaling deeply to keep my tears at bay.

I must have been convincing enough, because my friends smiled and laughed their way out of the car, grabbing their purses, rushing through the front door.

I hesitated before going inside. Standing on the doorstep, I'd never felt less like myself. Alarmingly cartoonish, I looked as if I'd tripped out of a line of fun-house characters, my dark brown skin serving as a harsh contrast to someone else's idea of beauty.

———

How often do we subject others to our own standards? Standards of beauty, healthy living, femininity, or masculinity? What shadows have we cast on one another by pulling out our diet and exercise routines, our religion and politics, as palettes of promise, showing the person in front of us what's possible if she'd just close her eyes and try it?

I was willing to try for the sake of fitting in. I was willing to prove myself adaptable, as one of two brown faces in the party crowd, to show that I was game to play by someone else's rules. I look back now and realize how easily I was swayed. I wasn't proving anything. I was sacrificing my confidence—letting someone else brush over my definition of raw, blank beauty, trading it in for something that falsely brought out my eyes. But I didn't see anything more pronounced than my shame.

If *I'd* chosen that shadow, it would have been different. I would've been making my own statement with bold color and daring fashion, like many chocolate-skinned girls I'd seen doing their thing and owning their personal expressions of beauty. But I didn't choose it. It was chosen for me.

If we're not careful, the temptation might be to suggest innocently—or even excitedly—that what works for one will work for all. If we feel good in blue shadow, if we feel our best at this weight or in these clothes or on this diet, if we feel personally validated by the way we vote or pray, then maybe everyone else will too.

But if that were true, perhaps we'd all be walking around in teal shirts and blue shadow, some of us looking and feeling like clowns.

The beauty in our uniqueness isn't best shared by forcing it on others, essentially brushing small strokes of blue eye shadow across someone else's way of life. The beauty is in seeing what's already there before us, whether basic or brilliant. When we recognize the value that already exists in a given life, we can marvel at the goodness of our Creator, who chose to make you and me a particular way for a particular purpose. Our work is to learn how to stand in awe of each created being without making modifications or trying to bring out something that's not ours to call forth.

We need to be cautious when what's true for us isn't true of someone else's life, avoiding the conclusion that it's not just that we differ or respectfully disagree but that their choice makes them unrelatable. Over time and left unchecked, the label "unrelatable" can morph into "other," and "other" into "inferior." Before we know it, we've turned preferences into presumptions, entering into one another's space without regard for how others have chosen to embrace and display their inherent worth.

Perhaps you've chosen to adapt as I once did, ignoring your own choices in order to fit in. Or maybe you find yourself reflecting on the ways you have unfairly and without permission imposed your choices on someone else. Forgiveness is available for the choices we've taken away. Hope is not lost, for we all can choose a different path going forward. I don't think we hear that enough: you can choose a different path. We can apologize for the ways we've forcefully compelled others to adopt our preferences, even preferences we believe to our core. We can sit on our hands and resist the impulse to perfect or modify what's already worthy as we remind ourselves that we can plant seeds but we can't force them to grow.

Maybe your work is to speak boldly about what's true for you, even if that means you remain makeup-less and minimal. Maybe your work is to speak your choice: whether of conviction or faith or expression. But perhaps your work is to ask for forgiveness, to listen, to let others choose what they feel is best. After all, the worth of every living being should be free to shine forth without the threat of someone else's shadow.

9

Jack and Jill

(Belonging)

Jack and Jill went up the hill
To fetch a pail of water.
Jack fell down and broke his crown,
And Jill came tumbling after.

—Traditional English nursery rhyme

I didn't realize my parents had paid for me to have black friends until much later in life.

Well, they didn't pay for *friends*. Rather, they paid for me to have the opportunity for structured activity time with other black kids like me—kids who were caught between the struggle of the black experience in America and the overwhelming whiteness of the environments we frequented.

This specific group of black friends, who came from families that had similar money and drove similar cars and lived in similar homes in similar suburbs, were part of a group called Jack and Jill of America Inc. The group was started in 1938 by twenty black mothers who wanted their families to stay connected after moving to predominantly white suburbs in Philadelphia.

Over the years, however, the group got a bad reputation for being overly exclusive. New members had to be invited to apply by a current member, which many blacks felt perpetuated the system of segregation but within the black community. To make matters worse, the black community started noticing similarities in how members looked and lived: many were upper middle class and could pass the "paper bag test," one method of unofficially assigning social status to blacks based on skin color. You were able to pass the test if your skin was no darker than the paper bag. In many cases, having lighter skin led to both blatant and inconspicuous instances of preferential treatment and privilege. It seemed the lighter your skin, the more acceptable—and accepted—you were.

I couldn't pass a paper bag test.

My very first Jack and Jill meeting took place in our chapter's clubhouse—a gazebo-shaped building just a few neighborhoods over from mine that was flooded with early morning light coming through the high, vaulted windows. At fourteen, I felt both skepticism and hope, similar to the feeling you get when trying a new hair product or nail color.

Looking around the room, I observed a few of my new chapter members: a tall, sturdy chocolate-skinned guy with a short fade who looked like an athlete; a yellow-toned girl with a perpetual pageant smile; a medium-toned girl with big brown eyes and an unimpressed face who looked *thrilled* to be there. My eyes darted from face to face, scanning the features of each black teenager.

In that moment, I was overcome with the unexpected and sobering realization that this group was different from my AAU track friends. I'd expected to feel excitement at the thought of getting to know other kids who looked like me. But in that moment, my hope was overshadowed by an ever-so-subtle awareness of what separated this new "us"—this room of black suburban kids—from the "us" that made up my Houston Sonics crew on the South Side.

What separated us was money.

I don't really know how much money my track friends had. It didn't matter. The beauty of suiting up every Saturday for track meets was that we proudly paraded around in the same purple-and-orange tracksuits, regardless of what neighborhood we were from or what our parents did for a living. There was unity in being a team—a unity that was predicated on skill and the achievement of common goals, not on what you looked like or what car you were driving out of the parking lot.

In this clubhouse it was clear that money mattered. The evidence came from the smallest of tells—hushed and half-concealed giveaways that let me know immediately who this group was for. As I continued to scan the room from my post at the door, I saw dollar signs as I registered the labels on kids' shirts, a girl who had bleached teeth, and her friend who was wearing a new set of orthodontia. Boys wore chains around their necks and wristwatches that bent the sun's light beams back onto the clubhouse walls in rainbow prisms. As I smelled the fragrances of cologne and fresh hair product, I just knew.

Money mattered here.

As I attended more meetings at the clubhouse and then teen conferences and serving days at soup kitchens, I grew comfortable with my Jack and Jill friends. Without having to explain it in words, we knew what united us.

We knew we were all going to the same cluster of suburban or private schools. We knew that most of us had our own (nice) cars. We knew that some of our parents were teachers, business owners, doctors, lawyers, and corporate professionals. We knew we shopped at the same stores at the same malls.

We knew which colleges we wanted to get into and that we were expected to make certain grades and get certain scores on our standardized tests so we could go to those schools. We listened to the same music; we had similar stories about being the only one in the room or the class or on the field or court that looked like our version of "us."

We knew on the inside what's so hard to say aloud and admit today: We were the "chosen" black kids. We were the black kids who were invited in—good enough to be a part of someone else's club. We were the kids who were clearly going somewhere—the ones who were undoubtedly going to do something with our lives. We were the crème de la crème, the well behaved, the high achievers, the kids of parents who'd "made it." We were acceptable—and accepted.

In the late '90s, the approximate yearly cost of chapter dues for Jack and Jillers across the country ranged from around two hundred to four hundred dollars, depending on the chapter.[7] I know a portion of that money was reinvested in the community. I know we spent our time serving others and giving back. I know the unnamed and unthreatened sameness to which our parents' money gained us access birthed many invaluable friendships. Some kids probably networked their way to their dream job because of their involvement. Without that community, I more than likely wouldn't have met my best friend, the friend I'd later take to prom my senior year and whose wedding I'd witness on a beach in Florida thirteen years later. And I know my parents only wanted me to feel comfort and acceptance in the company of black friends who were thrown into similar choppy waters. They wanted me to feel the camaraderie of navigating between our black heritage—of which we were confident and proud—and the white world within which we were trying to prove ourselves with our brains and our Benzes. We could climb our own hills to fetch our own brand of black, upper-middle-class success.

Still, that camaraderie cost them. Acceptance costs a pretty penny when wrapped in the translucent shroud of exclusivity. My parents were willing to pay that price for my sake, to secure belonging for me.

———

What's acceptance worth to us? What price are we willing to pay to fit in, to say that we belong? That we're not alone and can make it to the top?

For some, that price may be jail time, the cost of selling something in order to be part of a family that would do anything for us.

For others, that price might be Botox or a boob job. Some may be willing to pay too much for a new pair of jeans or the right workout pants.

Cars. Country clubs. That new iPhone and a cool Instagram story. Premium coffee, Pinterest boards, and good wine. Equestrian and swimming and soccer lessons. Highlights and a new haircut. Fresh Jordans or a flat bill. The highest bidder at the black-tie gala. Sick beats on the street corner's rap battle.

Jack and Jill. Membership dues. Exclusive invitations. The truth is, we've all fought the temptation to pay our way to the top of the acceptance hill in one way or another—whether we've realized it or not.

I couldn't pass the paper bag test; my skin was too dark. But it didn't matter because although I was the dark-skinned minority in a sea of minorities every year at teen conference, whether in Jack and Jill or as part of the Sonics track club, money initially opened the door for me.

Sometimes I still wonder what my having been a part of Jack and Jill means for me today as a woman, since I now have kids of my own who are growing up in mostly white spaces. I'm not a lawyer or a doctor. I'm not swimming in money. My kids haven't received an invitation to belong to a local chapter. I'm not sure how I'm going to open doors for my kids to be in community with other kids who look and live like them without playing into exclusivity. It's a seemingly impossible task for a parent—trying to love your kids well without opening them up to the unintended and potentially negative consequences of decisions made in their behalf.

In talking about my experience with my parents, I have come to see that they certainly didn't mean for my time in Jack and Jill to be about exclusivity. But by its very nature, my acceptance was cemented in the thick of separation from the start. My track friends exposed me to one facet of my blackness; my Jack and Jill friends, another. My track friends showed me the beauty and rawness of one world, while my Jack and Jill friends showed me the beauty and comfort of another. My parents wanted both for me.

I still look back on my time in this organization with profound fondness and gratitude. Regardless of how much I wrestled in the tension during my years there, without Jack and Jill, I wouldn't have entered into some of the most meaningful relationships in my life. I learned invaluable skills, like networking and teamwork. My love for service had plenty of places to blossom as we engaged our community. I truly believe my parents' deepest hopes for me were realized, because Jack and Jill played such a formative part of my adolescence.

Today, I wonder what I'm still willing to sacrifice for my own acceptance. I wonder what I've inadvertently asked of those close to me in order for them to belong in my life. Am I asking for the dues of loyalty and consciousness? Am I asking them to believe in certain values and raise their kids a certain way? What's the price tag for someone to belong in my home and heart? What's the price tag for someone to belong in yours? It's a hard question to ask myself and potentially even harder to answer if I choose to unravel the shrouds of exclusivity I've wrapped around myself.

I can imagine that Jack and Jill in the nursery rhyme were trying to fetch this pail of water together, trying to accomplish a goal as a like-minded duo, trying to make it triumphantly to the top. They probably lived similar lives, wore similar clothes, listened to similar music, and navigated similar stressors and relational hurdles. But when Jack fell down, Jill fell down too.

In time, maybe we'll come to understand that no matter how much we've paid to belong, human connection isn't found in the climb, in striving to belong. Instead, we actually find it in the shared pain of our falls. Authentic connection and belonging are fostered when we finally admit that we're part of the problem and that we've hurt someone or that we were wrong all along. Connection happens when we acknowledge that we don't have all the answers or that the established system may indeed be broken. When we can see others in their pain and stay there at ease and unoffended, connection and belonging result.

As I imagine it, either Jack or Jill helped the other up. They dusted themselves off and headed home, hand in hand, eager to patch up their wounds. They had nothing to show for their outing except a few bumps and bruises. No water, no proof of their ascent. At that point, I imagine nothing else mattered. They were just happy to have survived the tumble.

What costs have you incurred to belong? Whether it was your fraternity or sorority, your political party or your dinner club, you have likely sacrificed something of yourself. What did it cost you all those years ago when you just wanted to be noticed by *that* person? What is it costing you now to feel like you belong at the PTA meetings, the health club, the church service, or the boardroom table? Sometimes belonging is worth the cost, whether it's money or time or energy or hope.

But sometimes it's not. It's not worth it if we can't see one another at the bottom of the hill, after a fall. It's not worth it if someone lies there bruised and broken, cheated or afraid, unheard or devalued . . . and all we're worried about is the water.

10

Choreography

(Expectation)

No, it's 1-2, 3-4-5 and snap, tuuuurn, and lock." The muffled bass rattled from the boom box speaker as Ciara's "1, 2 Step" continued to echo through the living room of my girlfriend's house. The vaulted ceilings recycled the sound back down to the area in front of the couch where three of us were lined up in an orderly formation—not unlike Martha and the Vandellas or Diana Ross and the Supremes. I was definitely not Diana Ross. We had to start over.

"Ashlee, what are you doing?"

Every other word was interrupted by heavy exhales. Hands on the small of her back, my friend paused, waiting for my answer. I watched her for a couple of seconds as her chest rose and fell. It was clear she was tired—and irritated. We'd been at this choreography for a good thirty minutes, and we needed to nail it before next weekend's party.

"I don't know. I thought we were supposed to hit the lock and *then* the turn. I guess I just need to run it a couple more times."

The gravitational pull of the other dancer's eye roll was so forceful that it practically dragged her entire body to the ledge where the boom box was perched, its speakers looking like blissful insect eyes on either side of the controls. This girl was a friend of my girlfriend's—they'd known each other since elementary school. Her legs were long and sturdy stilts that supported her perfectly proportioned torso. Her face, punctuated with high cheekbones, was also long and framed by straight black hair that hit right above her shoulders. She had a name that looked like it should be pronounced one way but was pronounced completely differently—like how the Brits say *tomato*.

She didn't go to our private school, but she was popular. She was smart. She had a body made for dancing.

This girl took a sip of water after pausing the CD at the beginning of the track, stepping from side to side, shifting her weight as she whispered the lyrics to herself:

Automatic, supersonic, hypnotic, funky fresh (Ha!)
Work my body, so melodic, this beat rolls right through my
      chest . . . [8]

Hands on my hips, I bit my lip nervously, staring as she rehearsed the accompanying steps. I could tell she was serious.

"Okay, you ready?" my friend asked.

"Yup, let's do it," I said, more confidently than I actually felt.

We stepped back into our places as the track began. The electronic pulses began as producer Jazze Pha introduced Ciara—and we were off.

We swayed from side to side, dipped, and swung our arms with a snap. Then right leg, left leg, shoulder bounce, and twist back. The first verse was almost over, and as the transition to the chorus neared, my heart started pounding—and it wasn't because of the cardio.

Oh no.

My body paused in the lock position as the other two girls snapped and turned. In my paralyzed state, time slowed as I had an unusual flashback.

━━━

I was sitting in front of my parents' box-shaped big-screen TV that took up three-quarters of the wall in the family room. Feet propped up on the ledge, I watched in awe as I saw my little three-year-old body in pink tights and a short-sleeved black leotard lying on the floor. All the other girls were practicing their bridges, arched backs reaching for the ceiling as the teacher, who was wearing a sheer flowy skirt and scrunchy socks over her tights, went down the row to check everyone's progress. Most girls were squirmy, but they were focused and determined to arch their backs and please their teacher.

Then the camera paused on me. I arched my back for a split second, just before the teacher got to me. As she approached, I released the position and slouched down to a plank of careless defeat. She tried, for a moment, to help me back up—but I wasn't interested.

The tape continued, and it was clear that I was either too distracted or too curious to care about manners appropriate for the ballet. My energy was too demonstrative; my will was too strong.

━━━

No matter. Ballet wouldn't turn out to be my thing. But then I thought about the time I played—and then quit—soccer. Being the goalie in almost every game (coed, mind you) started to get real old real fast. I wanted to be a forward, dribbling the ball down the field, making flawless passes and scoring clutch goals for epic wins.

I thought about how I quit ice-skating because the instructor wanted me to repeat a class. I wanted to start practicing jumps—not shoot-the-duck across the ice for twenty minutes.

I quit gymnastics because I didn't like my coach.

Now here I was, considering my adolescent shortcomings and downfalls, the days that would never be described as "good ol'" or "glorious"—because I wasn't good enough for the studio or the field or the rink or the gym. Clearly, I wasn't good enough for the dance floor either.

Diana Ross and one Supreme were now sitting on the floor, arms clasped around their bent knees, huffing.

"Ashlee, we're going to try again—but this time we're just going to keep going if you mess up."

That was fair. I didn't want to be the one holding these two back from their greatness.

"That's fine. I'll practice when I get home."

We practiced the dance a couple more times. My form got a little better with each run, but one thing was clear after that afternoon: I wasn't a good dancer. At least, not a good hip-hop dancer, someone who could catch and keep up with someone else's choreography.

I drove home from my friend's house thinking about everything I'd decided to quit: ballet, soccer, ice-skating, gymnastics. Choosing not to pursue those sports wasn't a huge deal. I was young, and kids choose to quit things all the time. But something wasn't sitting well with me as I thought about how hard it was for me to learn that choreography—choreography that seemed to have come so easily to these other two girls.

As I pulled into the driveway, it sank in.

I turned the car off and sat there for a moment, overwhelmed with shock and a little bit of shame: *I'm black,* I thought. *I'm supposed to know how to dance.*

Ballet, soccer, ice-skating, gymnastics. Not knowing how to do those things didn't bother me, because I wasn't expected to know how to do them. Although I'd grown up seeing a handful of women of color dominating those sports in the Olympics and elsewhere, they were more the exception than the rule.

Hip-hop, though? Hip-hop was a black-girl dominated field—and it was hard for me. Not only was it hard, but I wasn't good at all. First rap lyrics, and now this. When was I ever going to figure this out? Would this ever not be a "thing"?

I got out of the car and went inside, ready to eat and get ready for bed. I felt at peace as I entered the house since I'd determined not to tell my parents about this revelation. It wasn't big enough to tell them, but it was significant to me.

Why wasn't I able to do something that I was supposed to know how to do?

The guys and girls at school dances looked to me and the other black girls to teach them new moves. When line dance songs played, people followed us. When the new hit from Usher or Kelis came on over the speakers, the chaperones would come a little closer as we coupled up with girlfriends or our crushes du jour to rock our heads and sway our hips to "Yeah!" or "Milkshake."

I realized that although others looked to me as the expert in certain environments, it didn't mean I was actually *good*. Had I tried that choreography in another group with different friends, I very well may have been laughed out of the room. Jerky arms, calculated steps—I was missing the je ne sais quoi of hip-hop. I was missing the essence, the ease that comes with love for the art and movement based in experience.

But I was enough of a typical black girl to lead the crowd at the private school dances.

What else had I learned to do just because someone expected me to know how? What steps had I carefully memorized as a part of my life's choreography—becoming good enough to make it in the different spaces where my body traveled: school, home, school, track—white people, family, white people, black?

I was moderately good at basketball and track—that was kind of expected. I liked rap music and played it loudly in my car—that was kind of expected too. But I also wore Doc Martens and spoke French and watched *Roswell*. What did this choreography tell people about me?

I'll never know for sure, but even though there was a lot I wasn't good at—things I'm sure people expected me to be good at—no one step, or even one misstep, ever represented the whole dance.

Luckily, I knew that even if I messed up our choreography at the party the next weekend (which I did, by the way), at least one of those girls would still be my friend. We're still friends to this day. Her expectations and frustrations were short lived—I'd like to believe because she knew there was more to me than what steps I could or couldn't land.

What was expected of you? Who were you expected to impress, or what were you expected to accomplish? When you fell short, what were the consequences? As frustrating as it can be to wrestle through the truth of who we are, what we're good at, what we're not, what we like, and what we can't stand—there's always more. We are more than the expectations other people have of us as mothers, fathers, bosses, and spouses. We are more than the expectations other people have of us as women, men, teenagers, and kids. As black people, white people, Asian, and Latino. There's more to us than these labels or categories. But we have to believe that if there's more in us, then there's more in everyone else too. The weight of expectation can be great. But as I've examined others' expectations of me, what's even scarier are the ones I may have unfairly placed on others. What limits or judgments have we unfairly placed on one another, given our own warped expectations?

Incidentally, unfair expectations are different from healthy accountability. We should hold people in positions of power and authority, or even people who've made commitments to us, accountable for their actions. Expectations that are congruent with position or promise are justified. I'm talking about the expectations assigned to us without our consent or knowledge, those dished out because of our looks or preferences or perceived abilities.

———

Years later, I took one hip-hop class right after I moved to Chicago. I was still pretty bad at it. But by then, I knew there was more to me, more to my womanhood and my blackness, than what people could see and judge from the outside. There was a thrill in the effort, but the effort didn't define me. I realized that any effort I attempted on my own would always be an incomplete part of the definition. The fullness of who I am, I believe, is wholly and completely found in Christ.

Whatever expectations have been unfairly etched into your movement, into the snaps and turns and locks of your life, take note of them. Know that they got there somehow, perhaps through someone else's voice or even your own. But those expectations aren't the only way to measure the fulfillment of your humanity. There are other beautiful, true, and rhythmic steps. There's more to be seen and known and loved.

11

The Senior Lounge

(Acceptance)

The wall above our lockers was filling up. As senior girls passed from the brightly lit reception area into the hallway containing their lockers, one could see the mascots and acronyms that represented our success: Yale, Harvard, Stanford, MIT.

Week after week, our school's college counselor would sweep out of her office, prairie skirt flowing wildly after, trying to keep up with her purposeful stride, her wispy brown hair perched atop her head like a bird's nest trying to survive a hurricane. Her eyeglasses straddled the very tip of her nose as she looked over her clipboard and then examined the wall, making sure there were no repeats.

At our school, whether girls were going to college wasn't really the question. The question was always "Did you get in?" closely followed by "Where are you going?"

It wasn't uncommon for us girls, as juniors, to apply to ten or more colleges and universities. Because money wasn't an object for the majority of us, many could spend $500 or more just to fill out stacks of paper that would be considered carefully by complete strangers.

As I thought through my desires and wishes for college, I was fully aware that I was privileged enough to make them a reality. My parents and grandmother were going to support my educational aspirations. The sky was truly the limit. If I could get in, I could go.

I dreamed about warm weather and being far away from home and on my own. I wanted to be able to find people who looked like me—but I also wanted to surround myself intentionally with people who were nothing like me, people from different countries who spoke different languages and had different skills and goals. I wanted to be proud of my college experience—not just academically but socially, spiritually, and emotionally as well. I wanted to get a degree I cared about and have a holistic experience that would challenge and change me, hopefully for the better.

I had assumed I'd major in business, since both my parents were sharp and successful businesspeople. My mother had earned her way into *Ebony Magazine* as one of the top black businesswomen in corporate America. My dad was an international salesman, with business that took him everywhere. If they had a knack for it, so would I. I'd work hard to build a worthy life that looked shiny and important and honorable, just like they had.

That's how I picked my list. Thirteen colleges and universities made the cut, ranging from the University of Florida to Pepperdine.

I was well trained. My counselors and teachers had stressed the importance of extracurriculars and leadership. So I led groups like student council and the varsity basketball team. Check. I needed to study hard to get good grades on my SAT and ACT. (Kind of) check. My overall GPA needed to be strong, bolstered by enough advanced placement classes for admissions offices to notice. Check.

I was well rounded. I wasn't getting into Harvard or Yale or Princeton, but I had what were, in my opinion, great and exciting options.

The most exciting option was the University of Southern California in Los Angeles. USC was my dream school, the one that made my stomach flutter with collegiate glee every time I thought about it. It was perfectly situated in a warm climate on the West Coast and boasted strong academics and a thriving cultural concentration of students who came from all over the world. Also, football. At the time, USC had one of the most talked about football programs in the nation. Check, check, check, check, check.

The fall of my senior year was stressful for us girls. With bated breath, we waited for early decision letters and fat welcome packets to drop on our doorsteps. Through the winter and spring, we started seeing girls roll into school with either triumphant smiles or stoic stares, trying hard not to show that they were so very disappointed. But mostly, there was positive news to report.

As the hallway wall became populated with Lions and Tigers and Bears, girls would run into the senior lounge across the hall to see who'd gotten into which school. That room belonged exclusively to twelfth graders—a place where gossip and good news flew out of the mouths of eager plaid-laden maidens, filling the ears of clique members and couch nappers alike. It was a safe space where seniors could take a break from underclassmen before and after school, during free periods and lunches. Didn't matter if you were a nerd or a nationally recognized athlete: all were welcome and all were wanted. If you were a senior, you belonged.

I'd gotten into nine out of thirteen schools so far. I hadn't gotten into Berkeley or Saint Louis University or Duke, which was okay because I'd gotten into the University of Miami, Tulane, and seven others. But I hadn't heard back from the final school, the one that mattered most: USC. It was April, nearing my birthday and the deadline when all schools were supposed to dish out their decisions, and I was growing anxious.

Finally, just before my birthday, I opened the front door after getting home from a long day. There on the brick doorstep, slightly cold and damp from the weird recipe of Houston weather, was a thick white envelope. It looked like it weighed as much as my laptop, bursting at the corners with papers that held my destiny. "If it's fat, that's a good sign," I'd been told. I knew from past yeses that my peers were correct.

I picked up the packet, took it inside, and ripped it open, eager to see the word I wanted so desperately to see: "Congratulations!" It was there. I'd gotten in.

Through tears, I celebrated with my parents that night. We now knew what I'd hoped for months. I was going to be a USC Trojan.

The next day, I sprinted past my locker to the senior lounge, yanked the round metal knob that was hanging on by half a screw, and burst through the old wooden door, backpack sagging to my knees. Out of breath, I scanned the room and saw that a handful of my friends were present.

"I got in! You guys, I got in!"

A chorus of cheers and applause erupted from the room. A couple of girls ran over to give me hugs. Everyone knew how badly I'd wanted USC. I'd put in the work. I was going to see my dream become reality.

After the celebration died down, I dropped my bag next to one of the round tables, ready to sit and look over some last-minute homework before assembly.

A girl approached me, someone I'd known since middle school whom I was cordial with but who was never part of my inner circle. I wasn't a part of hers either. Her bone-straight, strawberry-blond hair was perfectly parted down the middle. Without an introduction or morning salutation, she offered me words I wouldn't soon forget—words that would color my experience of work and success for years to come.

"You got in?"

"Yeah," I replied, with a slight smile, trying to play cool and authentically excited without seeming overly eager and arrogant.

"I didn't." There was a silent pause. I wasn't sure, in that moment, why she was telling me of her rejection. Did she want me to feel bad? Was I supposed to apologize? I started to speak, but what she said next clutched my unspoken word by the first letter and stuffed it back down my throat with an emphatic shove: "You know you only got in because you're black."

The room disappeared. In that moment, it was just her and me. Before I could open my mouth, she continued: "Yeah, the whole affirmative action thing. I didn't get in because I'm white. You probably got accepted just so they could meet their quota."

A girl next to me popped back into my periphery. She said this girl's name with a perfectly mixed cocktail of incredulity and disgust.

"Well, it's true," the girl continued.

A deep wave of wrinkles formed on my brow. I don't remember speaking any words, but in my head, I remember thinking twelve thoughts at once, each of them tripping over the others, trying to make it to the edge of my mouth.

Nothing. Here I was, standing in front of a different white girl. But we weren't in elementary school. And this wasn't innocent curiosity. I had nothing to say.

Shame wrestled my self-confidence to the ground: *You know she's right. You're just a warm black body to serve the university's statistics, to preserve their appearance as a culturally diverse institution.* But my confidence pulled a surprise move. *No, don't listen! She has no idea what she's talking about. She's salty and sad and is taking it out on you.* Then empathy tapped on confidence's shoulder: *Don't say anything snarky.*

She's clearly hurt. No need to add fuel to that fire. You care about her. Deep down, you do.

Fortunately, empathy won that day. Though my confidence was alive, it was bruised and limping. Shame walked off the court, waving its middle fingers at the crowd, but it had been there. It had put up a really strategic and well-fought match.

Finally, I mustered something that was true enough. "I'm sorry you didn't get in."

I realized in that moment that every girl in the senior lounge had paused to tune in. A vibrant hush harmonized with the bright fluorescents, and all you could hear was the hum of electric anticipation.

She stared at me for a few seconds more, emotionless, and eventually turned to head out to the hallway. I took a deep breath.

"That was messed up," a friend said from behind me.

Without acknowledging her, I turned my attention back to my homework. Slowly the room thawed, first into whispers and then into the normal soundtrack of lounge life: laughing, Beyoncé, the pitiful collapse of the rubber lining on the smelly fridge door as it received lunches for later.

———

Looking back, I'm not sure what was more messed up about that interaction: the hurtful words or the fact that those very words stuck with me far longer than they should have. More often than not in the years to come, when I was invited to lead or lend my voice, to show up and be seen, to speak in or out, those words played back like a warped cassette with pulled and twisted tape: *"Because you're black."*

Because I need to be seen to keep up appearances. Because someone else needs to look good.

Pain and rejection have the power to produce some of the most toxic and pervasive lies. Those lies can threaten our own sense of worth and humanity. Worse yet, those lies can make us believe that everyone else is devoid of it.

To this day, I still recruit every ounce of empathy and confidence I have to face the shame that tiptoes back onto the court, though it's getting smaller the more I see it. Each time I'm invited to lead or lend my voice, to show up and be seen, to speak in or out, I wonder to myself, *Why am I here? Why do they* really *want me here?*

But at least the lie can't hide. The lie is out in the open, and though it can still hurt and bruise, a lie that's in the light can be found by the Truth.

The lie that was there, out in the open in the middle of the senior lounge that day, was that the entirety of my worth could be reduced to a single part of me. That day, it was my blackness. I was worthy only because my blackness was, in someone else's opinion, the valuable piece.

There are lies that have tried to reduce you. To tell you that you're worthy only because you're a woman or a man. That you're valuable only because of your body or your brains. That the only reason you were accepted is the candidate you support or the cash you can count. You've been reduced down to your skin color or your sexual orientation. You've been diminished to your singleness or your special needs.

Some parts of our identities will hold more power than others. It absolutely matters how we use that power. But the truth is we're more than a single aspect of our identities.

On my way back to my locker from assembly that day, I passed by the wall across from the senior lounge. Three letters gleamed in crimson and gold: USC. Although for years to come I'd still wrestle with the lie that had been spoken over me, those letters represented more than just admission to a school.

Those letters represented the fullness of me, the fullness of my story when I was first thought of and dreamed about—accepted, wanted, valued. Not just by a human institution but by a God I believe in and serve, the writer of the story I was learning to hold and live.

"Congratulations!" I could see the word again as I closed my eyes.

Congratulations, indeed. The lies we tell and are told may live on, but they never have to have the final word.

12

Somerville

(Proximity)

I sometimes wonder who I would've become had I been raised around mostly black people—chocolate and cinnamon and sand-colored faces, many representing a motherland I'd never seen for myself—all knowing what is so hard to explain: that being black, no matter what your black looks, sounds, or thinks like, is a full-time job here in America. Trying to stay alive is an exhausting grind, regardless of your job or the car you drive or whether you have a college degree.

I think that's why, out of all my housing options my freshman year, I chose to live on the culturally black floor called Somerville.

I was certainly skeptical at first. Choosing to live with other students who identified as black seemed pretty exclusive—and I wasn't sure if the concept served or threatened my long-held desire to craft an intentionally diverse college experience. In addition, there was the embarrassing fact that other than my parents, track team, and Jack and Jill chapter, I'd never spent that much time actually doing life with black people before.

I was curious. Would I spend an entire year feeling completely out of place in a sea of faces like mine? Or would I find kinship among people who identified as I did, learning more about what others' blackness means to them, picking up new gems of culture and collecting them, like keep-sakes, to cherish and study for myself?

I took a chance and moved into one of the residence buildings that was nestled on the northwest side of USC's campus. That summer, I'd been communicating with a few of my suitemates, facilitating introductions and figuring out roommates and dorm assignments over a shiny new social networking platform called Facebook, writing on peoples' walls, and plotting inaugural floor parties.

There were thirty-two of us total: twenty-four girls and eight guys, the perfect ratio to almost pull off our own version of *The Bachelor*. We were divided into four corner suites, each suite containing a small common area with a kitchenette, a small bathroom, and four dorm rooms occupied by two students each. In the middle of all four suites was a lounge where we'd gather on stain-splotched couches for late-night talks about some up-and-coming politician named Barack Obama, Kanye West's latest album, the new Motorola Razr flip phone, the Lakers. There was some lounge drama when a strange, raggedy-looking man took naps there until campus police busted him, but, to my surprise, this floor of black faces was one of the most comforting aspects of my first-year experience. In a new state, at a new school, surrounded by so much that was unknown, this floor became what was most familiar.

I could come home from a long day of classes to two or three floor-mates who were crammed in my room, perched on plastic stools while playing my roommate's old-school Nintendo. I knew that once I stepped off the elevator and into our hallway, there was a good chance that at least two of the eight boys would be in their suite—the one across from mine—playing *Super Smash Bros.* or watching a movie. At least a couple of times a month, a group of us would make a run to Diddy Riese in Westwood for warm cookies and homemade ice cream or to Roscoe's for fried chicken and waffles. On game days during the fall, we'd make the trek to the Memorial Coliseum for Trojan football. The rhythm of life on this floor became a metronome for me, setting the pace and cadence for my coming and going. This community was easy, comfortable, and cozy, tucked around the corners of my life in college like a favorite wool blanket in wintertime.

Although their faces looked like mine, it became clear very quickly that our familiarity and connection wasn't only because of our melanin mix. It came in not having to explain why we black women tied our hair up with satin scarves at night or why we used lotions like Palmer's Cocoa Butter Formula for our skin so it wouldn't get ashy. It took shape in the wide range of music that filled the hallways and from the movies we watched to the magazines we read. Whether one of us was listening to non-hip-hop artists such as Kelly Clarkson or P!nk or to hip-hop, rap, or R & B, no explanation was necessary because there was an unspoken safety and understanding: *You don't need to try to prove yourself here.* If one of us was having a bad day that had nothing to do with a midterm or breakup and everything to do with microaggressions from one of our professors, we didn't need to spell it out. We were all aware of what existing as someone who looked like us could mean on the broadest of scales. We were connected, trying to make it unscathed through four (or more) years of an exemplary—and yet, by default, broken—experience within the system.

These students were musicians and architects, engineers and actors. They were Christian and atheist and biracial and bougie. Some were the children of single moms, while others had parents who were millionaires. This community of black students on our floor helped me realize for the first time that the hypothesis I'd been testing throughout my childhood— that there was one preferred or authentic brand of blackness—was false. There were infinite ways to don the crown of such a rich culture, myriad expressions of appreciation and understanding for the struggle of our ancestors, and countless hues on the color wheel of authenticity that all pointed to the sobering center of what it meant to be black. We were all trying to survive. All trying to live with honor and dignity and purpose on the shoulders of those slaves, immigrants, and scholars who'd gone before us.

The familiarity of Somerville was a firm foundation, a home base, and a shelter for the vulnerability of our aspirations and dreams.

———

One afternoon I came home from a long day of classes to chaos on my side of the floor. A group of floormates was gathered outside my suite door, and at first glance, I could tell some were more amused than others. A couple of the boys were against the wall, doubled over, mouths wide open to gulp in air as they attempted to recover from fits of laughter. Two of my suitemates were at the door, peering through a crack, attempting to get in.

"What's the matter?" I asked, letting my book bag slide off my forearm.

One of the girls managed a half turn, addressing me over her shoulder. "We can't get in."

"What do you mean you can't get in? Just open the door," I said.

"We can't," the other suitemate said. Irritation oozed from the end of her consonants as she shot a glance toward the two boys.

The girls made a space for me between them as I approached the door. I peeked inside, cracking the door open just a couple of inches before feeling its lower edge hit the side of a flimsy object. I heard the faint sound of a cup tip over and roll on its side and then the whisper of water slipping onto the tiled floor.

"You guys . . . Are you serious?" I asked, looking at the boys with a slight smile. I knew my suitemates weren't entertained, but I was picking up on the practical joke. "Is the whole floor covered?"

The boys nodded between new bursts of laughter. It was one of the oldest jokes in the book: the entire floor of our suite was covered in small paper cups, each one filled with water. If we were to swing the door open, water would pool over every part of the floor, making it impossible for us to get to our rooms untouched. There was no way around it: this was going to be messy.

"Y'all, I have to get to class!" one of my suitemates exclaimed. Her room was in the back corner, the farthest away and the hardest to reach.

"Okay, if we sacrifice a couple of cups, at least we can get the door open, and we can empty them out in the sink as we go," the other girl said.

"I have a couple of extra towels," I offered. "Let's do it."

Ignoring the background of snickers, one girl flung the door open with a decisive shove. Cups crashed to their sides, water running everywhere—slowly, but with determination, one puddle absorbed the next. For the next few minutes, the three of us wiped up the mess and emptied cups in our suite's bathroom, a few other Good Samaritans from other suites joining in on the cleanup effort. It took a long time, but finally the prank was undone.

"That was great," one of the boys said with a satisfied grin.

My two suitemates were annoyed, but eventually they were able to make it out with time enough to get to class.

That wasn't the end of the prank streak. In the coming weeks our suite would be the victim of swapped dorm rooms, where the boys took laptops, books, bedding, and accessories from a girls' dorm in the other wing and switched them out with similar items from a dorm in our suite. They also pulled a newspaper prank where they wrapped everything in our suite's common area in issues of the *Daily Trojan*.

After a while, these pranks became expected—endearing, even—and thus another brick in the foundation of familiarity was laid. The pranks were proof of just how close we'd become. Salty stares from the girls eventually melted into quick eye rolls and stifled smirks as we appreciated, over time, the careful planning and strategy it took to tease us.

Survival in the halls of Somerville had nothing to do with whether or not we were victims of odds that were stacked against us out there in society. Survival had everything to do with more lighthearted things like stackable cups and collegiate periodicals getting in the way of our classes and club meetings. Progress was deterred not by self-defeat and the energy often spent driving stakes in the ground of competitive climates but by welcome interruptions at the end of the day, those that told the story of our floor: we were fond of one another.

We were like those tiny plastic cups: stacked side by side, surrounded by other similarly positioned vessels filled with our own expressions of honor, dignity, and purpose. Sometimes we were able to empathize with what it means to hold the fullness of who we are, to keep it together, to be contained, managing the struggle of being black in America as our unpaid, full-time job. We knew how significant it was to be standing at all, not yet knocked down by the brutal blows of unjust systems, balancing on the breaths of our own voices, lifted by the potential of our sharp minds and sensibilities.

Yet our vessels were so different. Our bank accounts held different balances; we pursued different majors and championed different values. We'd had different experiences of love and loss; we'd seen different depths of brokenness and fracture in our families and neighborhoods.

But the beauty of my choosing proximity to a culture to which I'd questioned whether I belonged is that it helped me see more clearly both the gifts of shared experience and the power of individuality.

I didn't feel the pressure to be as artistic as my roommate or to go to law school like my best friend, but I could help hold their disappointments and they could help me make sense of my sometimes-messy journey back to myself.

I've come to find that the same is true for proximity of all sorts. Proximity draws us closer to the parts of our own stories we may have questioned or feared, allowing familiarity to wrap us up and bring us comfort without our protest and resistance. At the same time, proximity allows us to peer over the edge and get a better look at what each of us holds—our talents, our dreams, our hopes. And we can choose to honor them. We can dignify one another up close, calling out purpose and our unique stories, collecting them like keepsakes, turning them over and marveling at their majesty. Because there's something majestic inside everyone. Even if we're unfamiliar, even if they don't know it—it's there. Hope demands that we believe it's there.

When life gets tough—when we feel threatened by a news report or health scare or layoff—proximity means we can endure the weight of the crash together. Whether or not our skin shares hues of brown-gold tones, we can link arms and get to work, clearing the way for each of us to shine. Perhaps right on time.

But proximity also demands that we stay close when the shared experience doesn't reflect our own, when we're asked to confront the ways in which we've been complicit in another's pain. When we're tempted to be offended, proximity demands we stay put. Proximity isn't always pretty. But let me assure you, done well, it's pretty powerful.

This was the wonder of Somerville. Within the halls of a worn campus building on a culturally distinct floor, I realized I was fixating on the wrong question. I didn't have to wonder how I would've turned out if I had been raised around black people predominantly. The new question was, How do I stay connected to this beautiful heritage of which I'm a part? How do I stay close to my roots?

With either question, the old or the new, my experience would've mattered and the struggle of being me in America would've still been on my shoulders. The power of proximity isn't that it always removes the weight but that it reminds you that you don't have to carry it alone.

When's the last time proximity terrified you? If you've never been terrified, or at least mildly nervous, maybe there's a way to write some new questions of your own. The fear and potential for being offended that comes with getting close often exposes the part of our vulnerability we've worked so hard to protect. Walls come down. Barriers separate, and space is made for someone else's life or truth. Given our own convictions—the reasons why we are the way we are—removing walls and barriers can feel more like stripping down to our skivvies.

But whether it's by way of a dorm room floor or a dining room table, what's scary about proximity can also be the very thing that reminds us of who we really, truly are.

13

The Feast

(Perspective)

The rush of steam warmed my face as my friend lifted the lid. "This better be worth the wait," I said. A handful of us had made the long drive from Los Angeles to Arcadia, about a half hour outside the city, to wait in an hour-long line . . . for some dumplings.

"Oh, it's worth it, trust me," she replied. She took her chopsticks and quickly plopped two of the pork soup dumplings onto her plate.

The dumplings looked like little translucent Santa Claus sacks with a set of perfectly hemmed pleats atop each one, all swirling in parallel formation, meeting in the middle to form a flawlessly pinched tent. Ten of these dough purses slouched in the round bamboo steamer, the contrast of colors achieving a stunningly simple palette of natural hues: the muted yellow of the wooden tray beneath the delicate off-white of the parchment paper was the only backdrop. Add the cream-colored exterior of each dumpling, and you had a visual arrangement that suggested the most minimal of culinary efforts.

"This is it?" I asked, raising one cheek, unimpressed. I peered down into the steamer. I readied my chopsticks, hesitant. If a panel of *Chopped* judges saw this, there'd be no question who would be sent home for weak presentation.

Another friend, our chauffeur for the night, chimed in, "Ash, I could eat the whole tray by myself. You better get in there, girl!" He transferred four dumplings to his plate. As I watched him pop an entire dumpling into his mouth, I recalled our drive from campus to the restaurant: imagine every Bond movie meeting all *The Fast and the Furious* variations in one thirty-minute short film. White knuckles. Holding my breath. A whole lot of gripping the passenger seat handle and silently praying with sporadic pleas of, "Oh, God, please help me or this may be my last car ride ever." I was still a little shaky, actually.

I reluctantly loaded two dumplings onto my plate. Looking around the restaurant, I made my usual assessment, the one I conduct every time I enter any room: I was one of fewer than a handful of black people. My two friends, both Chinese, blended right in with a majority of patrons—and there I was sticking out like a new kid in a classroom. Again.

"Okay, here goes," I said. The dumpling swung from the tip of my chopsticks, its contents threatening to burst through the bottom and escape if I took too long.

I bit down into the dough. A thrilling burst of ginger soup filled my mouth, delightfully warming the back of my throat. The pork was tender and juicy. The exterior casing of doughy delight was soft, salty, and fun to chew. It was perfect.

"Oh my . . ." I began.

"Told you," my girlfriend said through a full mouth, moving a third dumpling to her plate.

We feasted on many different varieties, ending the experience with an order of red bean–flavored dumplings for dessert.

As we consumed the last dumplings, a question was put on the table for discussion. Up until that point, we'd talked Trojan football, Christmas break plans, and the latest news out of our campus Christian fellowship group, which was, according to our last group photo, 75 percent Asian.

"Okay, so what's everyone's spirit animal?"

"Spirit animal?" I asked.

"Yeah, like if you had to think of yourself as an animal based on your looks or mannerisms, what animal would you be?"

One friend answered, and then it was my turn.

"How about you, Ashlee?"

"Well," I started, struggling to talk through a mouthful of dumpling, "I haven't really thought about it before." A little bit of spittle escaped the corner of my mouth as I put up a finger, indicating my desire to finish chewing. My friends chuckled and moved along to the speed racer himself. Because he was good hearted but both fast and slightly reckless, I suggested that his spirit animal was a cross between a cheetah and a China-shop bull, mixed with a little bit of teddy bear for good measure. The conversation trailed off there. We paid and got ready to leave.

As we were getting up, I made it known that I definitely wanted to come back. "What's this place called again?" I asked.

"Din Tai Fung," my friends said in unison. As we made our way back to the car, they taught me how to say the name properly—inflections and everything. I felt official, as though I'd been inducted into a secret society.

We got into the car, full and satisfied. I felt proud that I'd tried something new—a culinary expedition I never would have chosen for myself had I not been acquainted with two regulars.

I took a deep breath and prepared myself for the Indy 500 back to campus. Except there were no helmets or checkered flags. Or opponents, for that matter. As we sped out of the parking lot, I was temporarily distracted by the music coming from the speakers. Unconsciously, I started bobbing my head and tapping my foot.

"You into this?" asked my friend who was driving.

"Yeah, I like it. Who is this?"

My girlfriend burst out laughing from the back seat, her distinct hoot battling the reverberation of bass. I always smiled when I heard her laugh, which was one of my favorites.

"What's so funny?" I asked, smile positioned, ready to be clued in. I was sure there was something to laugh about—I just wasn't sure what it was. All of a sudden, my full belly and the jerky lane switching weren't the most prominent part of the ride. A slow trickle of self-consciousness began to wash over me, starting at my head, making its way down to my toes.

One of them laid out the facts. "Well, we study at the twenty-four-hour Korean barbecue spot all the time. You just ate your weight in dumplings. You all of a sudden like K-pop . . . See a pattern here?"

A low rumble of laughter morphed into a full and free chorus that filled the entire car as we all realized my consistent and unapologetic affection for Asian culture. There was no reining us in. We were done for, the three of us drowning in a stupor of ab-crunching cackles.

For the first time, though, I didn't feel as if I had to qualify the conversation with a reminder to my friends—or to myself—of my *actual* race.

I could be fully proud of who I was *and* appreciate the richness of other cultures. I didn't have to forfeit one for the other. I didn't have to take off my blackness in order to like pork dumplings or listen to K-pop. I could hang out with my Asian friends and not feel like a sellout. I could hang out with my black friends and unashamedly recommend we go out for dumplings at my new favorite spot in Arcadia.

Before that day, I felt I had to tiptoe out of one world and into another. But that kind of posture, I realized, is laced with shame. It allows the "not fully enough" narrative to run rampant, terrorizing what is oftentimes the best part about sharing our lives with one another. The world around us is, by nature, divided into neighborhoods founded on classism and racism, into pockets of cultural monopolies that we secretly hope no one else will touch. We can play into that division, looking for safety over shared space, looking for quiet over connection. We can choose what keeps us fully comfortable and quarantined, preserved in the airtight containers of our own homes and holy church huddles.

Furthermore, if we do tiptoe into someone else's world, we may be tempted to feel as if we can't observe it up close without cheating on what's true of us. In that case, self-preservation wins, throwing up barriers and making someone else's life and culture tolerable, an experiment, but not in any way familiar.

We might lift the lid to see what's inside but fear what tasting a new pocket of humanity will do to us. Will it chip away at our pride? Will it threaten our power—the little or lot that we have? Will we somehow become diluted versions of our former selves?

Perspective can fully lift the lid off mere tolerance, exposing what we actually believe and think. With the right perspective, we see that one can be fully oneself *and* fully aware of God's hand on another life, culture, or way of moving in the world. We can be true to our own struggles and success—living in the shadows of the greats who've gone before us—*and* be marked by the spirit of someone else's goodness. We can hold both realities with utmost respect and without offensive appropriation, placing both lives on the scale and stepping back to see that they are equal.

In the safety of relationship or when an invitation is extended to us, we are then free to try something new. It was my friend who lifted the lid on the dumplings, after all. Upon receiving an invitation, we're free to immerse ourselves in the unfamiliar while suspending judgment of the other or ourselves.

That night in the car, I knew my perspective was shifting and healing in some small way. I could remain confidently in my place, proud and awake to my own story, a full owner of my heritage and history. But I could also feel the warmth of someone else's worth wrapped around me, like perfectly pleated dough. I was honored to have been invited to sit at the table, to witness what made someone else proud and whole.

When we have a healed perspective, others can shape us for the better without taking anything away. Maybe we'll recognize this perspective in one another instead of either insensitively adopting what wasn't ours to steward or remaining isolated and holding others at bay.

If we open up to perspective well, we may just earn the right to sit at someone else's table, joining in an expansive and fulfilling feast.

14

Two Big Macs

(Service)

It was winter in Los Angeles, which meant it was fifty-five degrees and sunny. A brisk and easy wind accompanied the sounds of the city: cars going too fast down Gladys Avenue, the echo of honking horns spilling over from I-10, the beep of trucks backing away after their morning deliveries.

As I stood on the sidewalk under an unmarked overhang, I imagined the students back on campus—girls in Uggs and short skirts; boys on their skateboards wearing Sperrys, khaki shorts, and hoodies—all with cups of coffee to warm their hands as they crisscrossed the quad in front of the hallmark Tommy Trojan statue. Since it was a weekend, most students were probably on their way to club meetings or study sessions or coming home from a late night on fraternity row.

From where I was standing, it was clear that winter necessitated more than cute furry boots and hoodies displaying school spirit. The contrast was stark.

Here in downtown LA, tucked between the Fashion District and Little Tokyo, I could see rows of tents and piles of trash. Members of the homeless population of Skid Row passed as they headed their separate ways: maybe to the Union Rescue Mission, a homeless shelter in the middle of the district; perhaps to the Los Angeles Mission to secure their first meal of the day and a shower; possibly to the Midnight Mission for the same.

I stopped watching so closely, my vision blurring and my mind drifting to the sobering reality that winter in LA meant many were cold. They were always cold, and they didn't have a consistent place to say.

After a few seconds, the present became reality again. I shot a quick glance to my left and right, watching the other students from my Christian campus group crack jokes and flash smiles at one another as they shifted their weight from side to side, trying to stay warm in the chilly shade.

"Okay, everyone, take your hats and socks and walk the block! For those of you who have meals, make sure we hand all of those out as well."

I looked down at my hands, each one holding a plastic bag from the local drugstore, both filled with solid-colored hats and socks. I was glad not to be handing out meals again, like last time.

As students were partnering up, my mind drifted to the last time we were here. We'd packed bags of chips and basic peanut butter sandwiches on cheap white bread in white Styrofoam to-go containers to hand out during the weekend, and the experience hadn't gone well for me. As I was giving one of the containers to an older black man whose temporary address was one of the downtown commerce buildings, he looked me squarely in the eye and respectfully—but firmly—rejected the meal.

"Do you have any meat?" he asked. "Something warm?"

"No sir," I replied. He turned his head to indicate that he was done with the exchange. I walked away, confused and more than a little self-righteous. At the time, I felt embarrassed and rejected. Later on, I realized just how ignorant I'd been.

"Why wouldn't he want food?" I'd asked my friend.

Having spent more time around the city's homeless population than I had, she looked at me with a knowing glance. "Sometimes, Ashlee, all they have to hold on to is their right to choose. All they have is a choice."

Her words stuck with me and rang loudly in the hollow space of my consciousness. Of course. In my privilege, I'd assumed that any meal was good enough. But not every meal was good enough. Would I have wanted PB&J on plain white bread? Not that day, I wouldn't have. So why would I expect anyone else to want it? Because they had less money than I did? Because they didn't have a home?

I was glad I was passing out socks.

My girlfriend and I paired up and started walking the block, heading southeast on 7th Street toward Central Avenue. We came across a couple of homeless travelers who were glad to pick out a pair of socks and a hat. A couple of people wanted meals; a few others declined.

As I tucked my scarf back into my coat, I consolidated the contents of my two bags.

"Which way should we head next?" I asked. I was feeling my usual depth of sadness mixed with anger mixed with loss. We'd done this a couple of times before. Who was I to be handing out these supplies to anyone? Was I any better off than the men and women who'd fallen into indescribably difficult circumstances, landing them here? My mind was spiraling down its usual funnel of despair. Why was it so cold? Why couldn't the LA housing market be cheaper? Why couldn't these missions and shelters serve more people? Why couldn't I do more to serve them?

We walked another half a block, handing out the rest of our hats and socks along the way. As we rounded the corner, a man caught my eye. He had a scraggly salt-and-pepper beard and weathered tan skin, and he was huddled in the corner between two storefronts.

He glanced over at the two of us and held my gaze for a while. It was one of those instances when maybe I should've been more cautious. But, for whatever reason, I felt as if his gaze told me just how tired and weary he was, how much he wanted rest—not just a break from the cold but from needing to survive like this.

"The rest of the group is out of food, aren't they?" I asked, not really expecting an answer.

My friend looked at me and then back at the man. "What are you thinking?" she asked.

"You know what? You go on ahead and meet up with the others. I'm going to go talk to him, and then I'll catch up with you guys before we head back."

She stopped in her tracks. "Ashlee . . ." she started. "I don't think that's a good idea."

"I'll be fine."

There was no way to know that what I'd said was true. But I felt in my bones that I was going to be fine.

I quickened my pace to a purpose-propelled stroll. Mema's words rang in my ears: "Walk like you're going somewhere," she always told me.

As I approached the man, he looked down, saying nothing. I left no space for him to acknowledge me, as I didn't want him to have to guess about my intentions.

"How are you today, sir?" He looked up.

"Sir, I know it's cold—and we just handed out the last of the meals we had. Can I walk you over to McDonald's and get you something to eat? Your pick."

He nodded once, then pushed himself off the wall, his wrinkled hands revealing traces of dirt underneath his fingernails and scabs that told stories of wounds that may have been more than physical in nature.

We walked silently, side by side, until we reached the shiny metal door of the McDonald's off Alameda Street. As we shuffled inside, I saw two of my friends across the street, concern spread large and wide across their expressions, like downtown graffiti. I offered a quick wave as if to say, *It's McDonald's. I'm not going to die.* And we disappeared underneath the golden arches, out of the cold and into the aroma of oiled and crispy french fries.

Second in line, I motioned to the board. "Pick anything you want."

Still, he said nothing. He gazed longingly at the backlit board, his squinted eyes bright with possibility. They darted from one menu item to the next, ping-ponging from the nuggets to the Filet-O-Fish, back to the nuggets, and then to the flurries. Finally, we inched forward, meeting our cashier face to face. Without looking at her, he said, "A Big Mac, please."

She paused, waiting for another item. But nothing.

"Will that be all?" she asked, looking at him, eyebrows raised in anticipation.

"Make that two," I interjected. "Two Big Macs, please. And a large fry." I didn't want fries. But perhaps he did. I'd let him decide.

We waited at the side for our food and then found a two-top table in the middle of the restaurant, the perfect spot for curious eyes to inspect and dissect the situation.

I had to admit we were an unusual pair. There I was, a black girl in her early twenties, bundled up from head to toe, and a homeless man. I watched him eat his burger as I tried to position my nose where I wouldn't smell the stench that started wafting from his outerwear. His mouth was rimmed with foamy spit that spread open with each bite. I thought he would eat quickly—four bites, tops. But he didn't. He ate slowly, deliberately, with utmost care and savoring.

I watched him, eating hardly any of my meal at all, but fully aware that I'd need to either eat it or wrap it up and take it home. Throwing any food away seemed like a really insensitive thing to do.

As he took his second-to-last bite, the man slowed his chewing even further and shifted his gaze from the ceiling to me.

Without words, he cracked a smile and then looked down at his burger.

I was growing uncomfortable—not with him, I realized, but with the silence. I wanted to know his name, his story. I wanted to know how long he'd been homeless—how long it'd been since his last meal. I wanted to know if he wanted any more to eat, if there was any other way I could help him.

Then, amid the buzz of kids laughing and playing in the PlayPlace, amid beeps from the deep fryer back in the kitchen and the soft rock tunes coming from the circular overhead speakers, I stopped.

Even with noise surrounding us, I heard a voice speak loudly to me: *Stay silent. You don't need to know those things. Just look at him. Just hold the space. Receive the gift of being able to hold the space.*

My throat tightened as I tried to hold back tears. They came all at once, without warning. I was mourning his circumstances. I was struck by my own pride—my need to know everything that wasn't mine to know at all. I was suddenly grateful for the gift of being able to provide without pomp and circumstance, with just two plastic bags and a van full of college kids.

But most of all, those tears made me realize that I was being served. I was the one on the receiving end of the nourishment of silence. I wasn't living in the cold, but I was desperate to receive the warmth of human connection. I wasn't hungry, but I was starving for space, for the comfort in knowing that no words are needed to experience the fullness of being wholly alive.

I'd assumed I was the one doing the serving that day. But in that moment, at that table, in the silence, I was overjoyed to know that a man

with nothing was giving me everything he had. He was giving me the gift
of his presence.

That meal was worth more than the four dollars I paid for it. Sitting
across from this unnamed, unknown man, "unusual" became ordinary.
"Stranger" became safe. "Homeless" became hospitable.

And I left that table with empty plastic bags but a full heart, bursting
with so much hope.

15

The Other Girl

(Audacity)

I regretted my decision immediately. As soon as I sat down, I decided my discernment must have been just as rickety and unstable as the table that kept rocking back and forth, back and forth—landing with a loud *thud* every time it came to rest by my right foot.

I could feel the blood start to drain from my face as the voices of my inner critics volleyed from one side of my brain to the other: *You should leave. No, stay. No, RUN, girl. Get outta there. Nope. Keep your bottom in that chair. Are you serious, Ashlee? You're seriously about to have this conversation right now?*

My foot started flying around in circles, my ankle holding on for dear life as it tried its best to support my twitch. I had a flashback to that one time my freshman year when my math professor called me out to let me know that my twitching foot was distracting and asked, "Could you please stop moving your foot like that?"

Well, I was here now. She'd be here any minute.

I took a deep breath, my nostrils sucking in the thick aroma of freshly ground beans. The whir of the grinder was suddenly just a lullaby of white noise compared to the persistent throbbing in my eardrums.

Around me, I could see students poring over encyclopedia-sized textbooks and stacks of printer paper slashed with brightly colored highlighter. A few were laughing loud enough to compete with the grinder. Jack Johnson was serenading the crowd from his invisible post in the ceiling—and a sea of black, white, and green reminded me that, as far as meeting places are concerned, this was as familiar as they come. There was some comfort in that. This place, across the street from campus, was familiar. The siren in the circle logo held the same faint smile, her hands positioned at the corners of her crown. She was mocking me. *You're nuts,* she was saying with her fixed gaze. *You're an absolute wacko.*

She's right, I thought. I had no business being here. What was this girl going to say? How would I respond? What were we going to talk about? Would we be here long?

The glass door at the far end of the shop swung open, its black metal trim blending into the backdrop of late evening. Time stood still as I realized that it was too late for me to bail. She'd see me any second. The girl glanced around quickly, checking the four-tops and the bar counter, shifting her shoulder bag from left side to right.

Finally, her eyes caught mine. I could tell she was hesitant by the way she pursed her lips when she finally found me sitting there. No smile—just a cordial nod as she made her way toward the seesaw table. She sat down with a long sigh, throwing her bag on the matching black metal ledge.

"Hey, girl, how was your meeting?" I started. *How was your meeting? That's the best you could come up with?*

"It was fine . . . Hey, do you mind if I get a drink really quickly?" She started for the counter, then paused to humor any dissent, should I have decided to offer one.

"No, go for it!" I answered, a little too eagerly. My voice was unusually singsongy.

"Okay, great. Be right back." She left just long enough for me to start breathing again, but I had no words. There was no good way to start this conversation.

She made it back to our table after a few minutes, doctoring up her coffee in silence. It was then I noticed just how unique her features really were: her jet-black hair maintained a slight wave and provided a stunning contrast to her clear, light eyes. Her skin was shiny, as if someone had taken a buffer to the top layer, ensuring that it was sparkling.

She was beautiful. I could see how he would've been attracted to her.

"So, what'd you want to talk about?" she asked, her stir stick forcing the cream deep to the bottom of her cup.

I wanted to disappear to the bottom of that cup too. I could feel my throat tighten. All of a sudden, it was very, very hot and I needed fresh air. I started with a fact. Facts were easy—indisputable.

"Um, well—I know you used to date . . . him," I offered.

She corrected me immediately. "No, we never dated," she said, glancing up from her coffee. "We just hung out for a while."

"'Hung out?'" Silence. I knew what that meant. Or, at least I thought I knew what that meant. My eyebrows were lifted, frozen in the middle of my forehead. My mouth was turned down as I considered her. "Okay, well, I just wanted you to know that I'm not holding anything against you. I know the tailgate party was pretty awkward the other day. Or, at least . . . people were trying to make it awkward."

She glanced up again, her bangs falling back to the side of her face. "Thanks," she said. "And, so you know, I'm dating someone right now. So I'm not even interested in him anymore."

"Oh, great!" I exclaimed. More eager singsong. "So, where'd you meet him?"

From there, she told me all about this new guy she was dating and how well their relationship was going. The conversation transitioned to her talking about her sorority and all the meetings she had to attend in the midst of finals season. We talked about our mutual friends and then eased into another moment of silence. To fill it, she picked up her white cardboard cup and knocked it back, emptying its contents from above her head.

"Well, thanks for asking me to coffee," she said. "I think I should be getting back to my apartment. I'll see you around?"

Surprisingly, we lived on the same street just east of campus but had never seen each other until a recent football game. Her presence had sparked rumors and gossip—most reported to me. I'd noticed how comfortable she'd been with him but tried to make nothing of her perfect teeth and her hand resting gently on his shoulder every time he made her laugh. A couple of acquaintances had told me they used to date.

The football game came and went, but I kept thinking about her. I imagined him wishing she were sitting beside him in the velvet seats at the movie theater. I imagined him holding her hand, helping her up the steep steps of the fraternity house. I imagined them laughing all the time as they had at the tailgate.

She became my opposition, with just a couple of glances and a few whispered words. She was the one to look out for, the one to tear down with sour and sarcastic smiles. She was the one to avoid.

After a couple of weeks, though, I saw her in one of the marbled hallways outside a lecture hall, and I decided to tell myself the truth: *She's done nothing to you but be herself—her charming, winsome, beautiful self.*

So I decided to defy the deadly stories that were being told about her, both the ones relayed to me and the ones I found I was telling myself. The one way I could think of to undo the damage was to look her in the eye and see her.

I'd reached out over Facebook and asked if we could get coffee.
She'd agreed.

"Thanks for meeting me," I replied to her as she shouldered her bag.
"See you at the next tailgate?"

"Sure," she said, flashing a quick smile. She turned and tossed her
cup into the recycling can with one swift sweep of her arm. Then she was
gone.

I sat there, stunned by how underwhelming our conversation had
been. It was quick and awkward and uncomfortable. In that moment, I
felt like a fool.

But as sweaty as my palms were, I knew I'd accomplished my goal—
the one she had no idea I'd set. I'd undone the damage. Walking in, she'd
been my opponent. Walking out, she was ordinary. She was an ordinary
girl who was extraordinarily likable. She had an edge to her, but it was
clear she was hardworking, fitting in responsibilities between games and
social engagements. She wasn't the malicious side chick I'd made her out
to be.

As I wiped my palms on my jeans, the voices returned.

You should've called her out about the tailgate.

Why? Why would that be necessary?

*Because that girl's still a threat! Did you see the way she was looking
at you?*

I closed my eyes, demanding the voices into silence.

This is the way we combat the damaging and deadly stories we tell
ourselves about others—the ones that have the power to turn ordinary
people into opponents, normal into nemesis. We combat the stories about
our roommates or our in-laws or our uncles or our bosses by silencing the
voices—by demanding that we see the goodness in others, or at least the
ordinary, however much or little we feel is there.

Doing this takes audacity—the audacity of meekness and truth, which tells us that we might be wrong. Even if we're not wrong about them, we're certainly not completely right.

That girl and me? We never became friends. But I'm glad I didn't let feeling a little foolish stop me from confronting the deadly story.

As crazy as it felt at the time, some audacity helped bring me back to her humanity.

16

Lunch Run

(Humiliation)

Being proximate doesn't always work out the way we want it to. The day was bright, the sun shining and holding the promise of another fulfilling weekday. I'd just started my internship at Human Rights Watch in downtown LA, giddy with excitement at the prospect of making copies, delivering mail, ordering supplies, and looking over the shoulders of some of the great advocates of my time: women who were fighting for justice in between phone calls to attorneys and hours of closed-door concentration as they reviewed new cases.

I loved having the chance to be a fly on the wall, witnessing both the constant rage and the delicate hope of advocating for twelve- and thirteen-year-old boys who were being tried as adults—because they were in the wrong place at the wrong time, because they didn't know better, because the color of their skin meant they were guilty, or because an older sibling blamed them instead.

This was an unpaid internship, but I had the privilege of holding someone else's armor on the front lines of this fight. In fielding phone calls at the office and preparing for events, I got to see powerful, smart women spend the best hours of their day asking big questions about broken

systems—such as why life sentences were being dished out to minors—
and then empty themselves of their energy and time and intellect to find
the impossible answers.

As a fly and armor-bearer, I decided I could do good by listening, by
showing up on time, by trying to keep our spaces neat and tidy, and by
staying out of the way when days were particularly tense.

But I was also looking at the future version of me doing good. I was
determined to become someone who would advocate and fight and uplift
and ask questions. I wanted to track down impossible answers and try to
make sense of them, allowing my discontent to fuel the vision of a better
future.

On this particular day, the warmth of the sun was enough to make me
want something cold and icy for lunch. Usually, I'd head downstairs to the
first floor of our office building with our other intern and grab a quick
sandwich or a soup-and-salad combo from the deli. But this day was nice
enough that I decided to walk the long mile to the nearest Jamba Juice.

I told my supervisor that I'd be back. She nodded without looking up
from her computer, most likely engaged in making sense of a long pile of
unanswered emails, each one clamoring for her attention and reply.

I took the elevator down to the first floor. Just a couple of weeks
earlier, I'd almost been stuck in that small, cramped space when an earthquake struck in the middle of the day, right around lunchtime. Instead of
going straight down to the deli, I'd decided to go to the bathroom and
then back to my desk for my wallet. At my desk, without warning, the
entire room started swaying, gliding first one way and then the other, as
if it were ballroom dancing on top of its roller bearings. Although I had
no official earthquake training, I instinctively huddled under my desk,
each hand braced on either side of the small opening that separated my
stash of sticky notes and paper clips from all the important documents
needing to be filed.

After a few seconds, the room stopped shaking and kept going at the same time. Our senior attorney said nothing, the *tap-tap* of her typing resuming from her hallway office as soon as the tremors died down. My supervisor asked if I was okay. Our other full-time staff person burst through the door, laughing, telling us how she'd been caught in a bathroom stall.

Now, as the elevator came to rest at the bottom of its track, the doors slid open with a *ding,* and I stepped out into the lobby. The glass windows hosted the infinite rays that were piercing through each pane, warming my skin.

I left the building and walked down the concrete sidewalk, my steps easy and light. Today wasn't as heavy a day as I'd experienced in the past, when my energy was focused mostly on planning our biggest fund-raiser of the year at the Beverly Hilton hotel. My mind drifted from work to school and back again. It was the summer before my senior year of college, and I found myself surprisingly reflective. I had only two more semesters to go before being catapulted into the real world—where no one hands you a schedule to follow or plans breaks between projects, where money is absorbed by insurance premiums and electric bills, where relationships you were so sure of are suddenly distant memories.

By the time I reached the front door of Jamba Juice, my skin was warm to the touch. As I crossed through the doorway and into the chilled entrance, my hair stood on end, shocked by the harsh transition.

I looked ahead. There was only one person in front of me ordering his smoothie, a pleasant surprise given that it was lunch hour on a warm day. As I craned my neck back to look at the menu board, a small movement to the left caught my eye.

Having decided on a medium Banana Berry, I felt free to take notice. There, standing not five feet from me, a woman was hunched over the juice cooler, rummaging through the selection of prebottled juices and smoothies. She wore a long overcoat, which I found unusual given the temperature outside—and it was filthy. It was covered in dirt and flecks of leaves, indicating that perhaps she'd spent more time reclining on bare ground than a typical Angeleno would. From time to time, she looked over her shoulder to see if anyone was watching.

After a few moments, I realized what was taking place. As she moved, the left side of her coat flapped up to reveal a reusable bag. The screw top of one of the bottles was peeking over the edge, its vibrant bright green giving her away. She continued stuffing the juices into her bag, one at a time.

I felt my heart sink to the bottom of my stomach. I was witnessing a woman take what she felt she needed—and yet she was taking it without permission. Everything in me wanted her to have that juice. I wanted to look away and pretend I hadn't seen her stealing, but I couldn't do that. But I was determined to make sure she got what she needed.

It was my time, I felt, to do good. I leaned to my left a little. In a hushed whisper, I started to speak. "Ma'am . . . Ma'am?"

No response.

This time, I whispered with a little more volume. "Ma'am?"

She turned around, startled, juice in her right hand. Her eyes were gray and glassy; her skin was irritated and inflamed with red splotches, perhaps exacerbated by the sun. She had short white hair cropped around her face in a disheveled bowl cut. She stared at me without a word, mouth slightly open and forming a small O, forehead wrinkled and revealing her skepticism. She looked as if she knew she'd been caught.

"Ma'am," I continued quietly, "just let me know how many juices you have in there, and I'll pay for them. Just tell me the number."

What came next nearly knocked me off my feet.

Her face turned bright red as she swung around to face me. "You think *you* know what's best? You NIGGER. You're nothing but a NI—"

It was as if her words were muted after that. Stunned, I saw her mouth moving in slow motion, as if she were standing four inches away. My vision blurred, and I felt myself blink slowly. I rotated my neck to look at the cashier, a young man with a deer-caught-in-the-headlights expression on his face. The man who was just in front of me approached the woman, right arm extended, trying to get her attention.

I came back to the present, slo-mo temporarily suspended. She was still yelling at me, but now the manager and another employee were escorting her out, taking the juices out of her bag as they led her to the door.

In a matter of seconds, it was all over. But her fury and the word she said had already latched on. It wasn't leaving any time soon.

"I-I'm so sorry," the cashier stammered.

"It's—" I couldn't say it. I couldn't say *It's okay.*

"What do you want to drink? It's on us," he said.

I must've managed to tell him what I wanted, because in what felt like no time at all, I was holding a large smoothie in my hand. The manager walked with me to the door and led me out, making sure I was collected enough to head back to my building.

"Are you good to walk by yourself?" he asked.

"I'll be fine," I said, forcing the words up through my throat and into the warm California air. The day didn't seem as bright anymore.

He hesitated, and I noticed him watching me until I disappeared around the corner. I waited until he couldn't see me—and then I let the sobs come. For the entire walk back, I sobbed. I didn't care who saw me; I wasn't paying attention anyway. I sobbed because this was the first time someone had called me that wretched word to my face. I sobbed because I was angry that I couldn't avoid it. I sobbed because I'd caused a scene and because this woman was forced to leave without the things she clearly wanted. I sobbed because I drew attention to her. I sobbed because I knew that as much as I wanted to secure justice for someone else, there was still some injustice lingering out there, somewhere, for me too. On the longest walk of my life back to the office, I realized that no matter how hard I tried to work my way up and out, no matter how shiny my degree or how noble the cause, no matter how impressive the position or accolades I earned, someone could always try to reduce me to just another "nigger." It was a word used to oppress for decades. I wasn't the first to be called one, and, sadly, I knew I wouldn't be the last.

Somehow I made it back up the elevator without remembering how I'd gotten that far, this time caught in the middle of my own personal earthquake. No one else was shaken except for me. I was undone, but all out of tears.

I slumped back down at my desk, my hand slowly letting go of my smoothie. It was then that I noticed my hand was shaking.

Our event coordinator must've seen me come in, because after a few seconds, she asked me if I was all right.

I don't know why, but I answered her honestly. "A homeless lady at Jamba Juice just called me a nigger," I said softly.

She stopped typing. Another one of the women came from around the corner and stood at the intersection between her hallway and my desk.

"Ashlee, I'm so sorry," she said. There was stillness and silence—held delicately by the three of us—for a lot longer than I would've liked. I appreciated their concern, but I didn't want anyone to be sorry: not her, not the cashier. Deep down, I wanted them to fight as hard for me as they were fighting for incarcerated minors. I wanted them to feel as shaken and taken aback as I'd felt—knocked completely off their feet. For just one holy moment, I wanted them to feel crushed and paralyzed and enraged and grieved, all at the same time. But I knew they couldn't—because they weren't me and they didn't have to.

So I said the truest thing I could say: "Me too."

Slowly, the typing resumed. The other woman pivoted, arms crossed, and walked back to her desk. And life continued.

Humiliated, I went about my day, doing as much good as I could for an afternoon—filing old reports and answering calls and sorting supplies. But I left that day knowing that sometimes even doing good is not enough. Sometimes we just have to sit with what's hard and humiliating about the difficult work of unity and do our best not to let it kill us. Instead, we need to let it shape us in some other way that sobers us up and forces us to take off our rose-colored glasses, to admit that sometimes moving closer and trying to do good and closing the gaps between us and others doesn't work out the way we want.

But maybe it's worth showing up anyway. Maybe we still show up just to prove that kindness and proximity aren't always about our comfort. We keep showing up to remind ourselves that dignity and hope weigh more than humiliation's sting.

17

Cake Toppers

(Friendship)

The cake sat on the bistro table, the three figurines on top posed like mannequins, stuck in the same positions and boasting the same red-lipped grins. One was an olive-skinned girl with a straight black bob. She was supposed to be Emily, who in real life had longer, silkier black hair and a face that was exponentially more attractive than her figurine's. The other two were identical, both chocolate colored and wearing the exact same bob. One represented me. The other represented my friend Lauren. We, too, were more attractive than the little wax girls. Three figurines wearing graduation gowns, representing the three of us: the college friends who finally graduated with our friendship still intact.

As I sat on the bench looking at the cake, memories like scenes from old movie reels swept across my mind. These were the two who stayed by my side over the course of four long years, in spite of my faults.

———

I thought of our first year together when I was determined not to fall into the looming trap of the infamous freshman fifteen—the curse that befalls many eager first years after all-nighters mixed with unlimited meal plan access, when Thirsty Thursdays or Three-Dolla Hollas eventually compromise one's toned tummy, slender hips, and expansive thigh gap.

I'd gone home for one of my first school breaks, and I remember my dad asking me if I was eating. During those few days, my parents fed me smothered pork chops with white rice and cornbread, and Uncle Sam's ribs with greens and pinto beans were piled atop my plate as if my parents were not so subtly hoping I'd gain some weight.

Without really realizing it, I had been holding the hope of maybe one day fitting into the LA scene—gripping it as tightly as I held the bars of the elliptical in the school gym, hoping to be skinny and pretty and fashionable enough to keep up with the girls who effortlessly hung out with the athletes and the frat boys.

So I traded in my soul food for dainty plates of egg whites mixed with spinach, a little bit of cheddar, and a whole lot of nothing else. I trekked across the walkway from our dorm to the workout facility twice a day almost every day—before my first class and after my last one.

I was withering. But the two girls on top of that cake didn't let me wither all the way down. They helped me loosen my grip, gently and one finger at a time, reminding me of who I was by offering to walk with me to Bible study with the assumption that we were going. They made sure my inner foodie stayed fed, occasionally inviting me out for sushi and coffees and In-N-Out and ice cream. They cracked silly jokes, made sure I laughed, and helped me keep my hope focused on the things that really mattered.

And when I became too focused again on the hope of LA, they were there to look me in the eye and remind me, once again, that I was enough.

———

One time, while watching a movie in the boys' suite on our floor, I sat cross-legged in my baggy USC sweatpants surrounded by my roommates, settled in with a pint of Häagen-Dazs. Lauren was sitting next to me on the couch, her Häagen-Dazs in hand. As the movie progressed, I took one small bite and then another. We all laughed at the funny parts, mouths wide, creamy pools of milk and sugar melting in our mouths. The movie was too good to get up and take a bathroom break, so there I sat, relaxed and happy, surrounded by some of my favorite people.

Too soon, the movie ended. As one of the boys got up to flick the suite light back on, I reached my spoon into the cardboard carton to take one last bite. Laughing at something someone said, I tilted my head back while simultaneously going in for the scoop.

Nothing.

I tried again, this time looking down into the hollow of the pint.

The white plastic of the spoon met the white cardboard of the base, and it was then I realized I'd eaten the entire thing.

My mouth slid open in disbelief. The tears followed.

I called my friend's name, softly at first. She wasn't paying attention, so I elbowed her sharply.

"Ow! Ashlee, that hur—wait, why are you crying?"

"Because I just ate over one thousand calories' worth of ice cream, *that's* whyyy!" I sobbed.

Everyone in the suite turned their attention toward me, concerned gazes shifting from my empty pint to my snotty face. A hush came over the space. A few people shuffled out quietly to escape the awkwardness, their slippers giving them away. The guilt took my body hostage, sharply, like brain freeze.

After a few moments of pity, I turned, bleary eyed, toward my friend.

Her smile was wide, her bright teeth meeting my sobs with light-hearted optimism.

"Why are you smiling? I just ate a *whole* pint of ice cream in one sitting!" I demanded.

The guilt turned to anger. She of all people would know how this messed things up for me.

Without a word, my friend tipped her pint of ice cream toward me. As I leaned over to see what was inside, I saw another hollow white cardboard space where her ice cream used to be.

I looked back at her, and after a short pause, she keeled over and let out a long, drawn-out holler, allowing her pint to roll off her fingertips and onto the tiled floor as her laughter rolled away with it.

At first, I did nothing, holding my face in a scowl, resenting the fact that she wasn't taking my poor nutritional choice seriously.

But as she so often did, she softened me. After a few seconds of hearing her laugh, my scowl shifted to a pout and then a smirk, and finally I was laughing too. The salt from my tears fell onto my tongue, and I kept laughing. The few people left in the suite unpaused, resuming their journeys back to their rooms, a few of them laughing with us, one person whispering under his breath, "Y'all are crazy."

We laughed until our stomachs hurt—or maybe that was from the ice cream—and we laughed until I had to cross my legs to keep from leaking in my sweatpants.

Staring into the now-lit candles on the cake, I smiled faintly. Time and again, these girls had reminded me in more ways than one that in spite of my rigidity and self-loathing, my image consciousness and my striving, my true self was usually found when everything else had vanished. When I looked up and found myself empty, there they both were, waiting for me to see that not only was I fine, but I was alive and well.

Still smiling, I looked over to my other friend, the one with the olive-kissed skin. She was relaxed and comfortable in her spot in the booth, observing our parents, siblings, and friends as they shuffled around the tables, moving among the three of us with ease.

———

I remembered when we attended our Christian fellowship retreat at Campus by the Sea on Catalina Island. The two of us sat in the circle of old blue conference chairs with silver edging. In a sea of tan, olive, and peach-colored stones, I was one of fewer than a handful of rounded black pebbles staring back at the others across the circle from me, seeking community and a place to belong. I'd taken a chance and had crossed the smallest sliver of the Pacific to be there, and now I had my guard up.

But Emily was there with me. My friend made sure I knew peoples' names and knew where to be at what time. She saved me a seat next to her. All of a sudden, I was the new girl in every teen rom-com who transferred in the middle of the school year—eyes darting, surveying the faces of those with whom I was supposed to go deep and ask questions and process my life in the context of faith.

I could risk in that environment, bravely stepping in—an island on an island—because she was there.

At one session the weight of exams and exploring a new tribe of people must've been too much for me to carry. Around this circle, we were praying. After lunch. You should never schedule a contemplative prayer session after lunch. With my head bowed, my eyelids flew open and fluttered shut on repeat, the spell of pizza and salad and tater tots completely disabling whatever function it is that keeps you alert during prayer time. I opened my eyes again and saw the blurry golden block letters on my red sweatpants: $U \ldots S \ldots$ and then, blackness.

In what felt like no time at all, I woke up to snickers and stares. My head was tilted, comfortably secured on a soft pillow-like cushion. As I took in the circle once more, I could tell that no one was praying anymore. They were all looking at me.

I sat straight up, startled and horrified by the sudden recognition that, yes, I'd fallen asleep during prayer time. (I mean, let's be honest though, who hasn't?) Wondering what surface I'd found upon which to rest, I looked to my right, and there she was. Red faced and wide mouthed, my friend could not be contained. As her signature laugh interrupted the hum of the old AC units, I looked down at her shoulder and saw a darkened splotch of spittle, mocking me from its post.

"Good morning, sunshine!" she started.

The room erupted, and I couldn't help but crack a sleepy smile myself.

━━━

Looking across the table once more, I thought back to that moment and realized that she could've elbowed me awake. But she didn't. Not out of spite, I realized. She knew what I needed, and she made a space for it. That space, as with many other spaces she'd create, was her own offering of self-sacrifice: her shoulder, her dorm room, the seat next to her that could've been easily occupied by a backpack or stack of books.

As the wax figurines began to melt, I realized how grateful I was, not just for the gift of their friendship—friendship that had shown me what it means to share burdens and shoulders, to laugh and lighten moods, to not allow a pint of pity to ruin the whole purpose of the adventure in the first place—but for the fact that it was a gift I was excited to return.

So much of how we see others, how we uplift and uphold the people around us, is stenciled by the company we've kept and choose to keep.

The people we call friends are the people we feel known and seen by—who make us better and call us higher. These are the cake toppers, the ones who stand next to us when we cross the finish line, when it's time to celebrate and embark on a new chapter. But they also shape and form us, and they help us look at the world around us as rich with spaces that call out "full," "safe," and "possible." They teach us how to look at our own silly quirks not as immature adolescence but as evidence of our truest selves. They teach us the way forward—toward embracing our humanity versus moving further away from it. Sometimes they teach us how to confront it, to let the unhealthy and unhelpful parts die so that better life can rise strong in us.

Perhaps the way we learn to see and dignify complete strangers starts with the way we learned to define *friend*. How we define it—whether based on who picked us for kickball or who dressed like us at school or who shares our interests, temperament, or status—inevitably makes its way into our definition of dignity.

Today, perhaps we define *friend* the same way we did in second grade. But maybe some of us have cake toppers: people who've called us out and up, who've pushed us to do our very best, who've seen us at our absolute worst and still believed in us, who've told us the truth about ourselves, even when it hurt. These are the great friends, the friends who sacrifice and know what we need, who make us better. Not just for ourselves—but for the world.

I'm glad I had Emily and Lauren during some of the most formative years of my life. They were two bright flames pointing me back to myself in the big, sometimes dark, place that is LA. They helped show me how to be kind and patient with myself. I'd like to think that because of them, I am also better for the rest of the world.

Because of them, I realized I don't just want kickball friends, the ones who come and go and never call me to anything greater. Frankly, the time is past for that type of companionship. The world is a big, sometimes dark, place—and we need people around who will help us find and be and spread more light. We need challengers and safe havens and joy givers and truth tellers. We need lovers of justice and mercy. We need reconcilers in our corner. We need the people who at the end of the day, when the four years (or four decades) are done and we've got the scrapes and success stories to show for it, will be there, standing tall by our sides, shoulder to shoulder, reminding us that pure joy may live at the end of a plastic spoon and that rest may be found on a willing shoulder.

18

Thanksgiving

(Gratitude)

I remember when I first met him. He towered over me in the quad, his tufts of sandy-brown hair yielding to the gentle fall breeze. I remember it still felt like summer, even though the fall semester had begun. A couple of other freshmen were there too, but he was one of the only guys I remember from orientation.

I remember him being kind and gentle, a little bit quirky and refreshingly quick witted. Truth be told, it seemed from our first few conversations that we were both in silent agreement that we would be friends.

Our friendship seemed to come easy, a rare and unusual occurrence for freshman year. I'd thought making friends would be harder, and in many instances, it was. Not with him, though. Which made me a little skeptical. I was confused by his amicable approach.

He's a tall white Jewish guy, I thought. *Why in the world would he want to be friends with me? On purpose?*

But he did want to be friends. And I'm really glad he did.

We'd occasionally grab lunch in the center of campus. Or we'd find ourselves hanging out with his friend, the two of us serving as the very normal backdrops to his friend's lavish and luxurious lifestyle, complete with private jets and quick trips to Vegas.

We talked about my parents and my childhood in Houston, about his family and growing up on the East Coast. We talked about his little brother, and, after graduating from college, we talked about his sweet mom's battle with cancer.

In many ways, he was my Switzerland: the neutral, safe, and comforting ground I found in the midst of the collegiate crazy. I could process the woes of flunking Business Accounting and trying to decide whether I would seek to join a sorority. I could be my unimpressive self, the one who craved the combo from Del Taco rather than the club scene downtown. With him, I could simply, happily exist.

Perhaps because our friendship was so easy and safe, a few months in I thought, *Why not?* and I invited him to join my family in Texas for Thanksgiving. That threw everyone for a loop. Because apparently you don't just invite a guy home for a holiday unless it's something, you know, *serious.*

"Are you dating?" "Who is he?" my friends and family inquired.

"No, we aren't dating," I said matter-of-factly, more than once. "He's my friend." We were simply enjoying the benefits of the purest, most disarming form of friendship. To this day, I've never experienced anything quite like it.

Why does pure friendship seem so rare? We're usually more loosely acquainted, or we exist in the same social circles, or we jump to being romantically involved—with few, if any, in-between alternatives. Why do we miss out on the kind of friendship that is intentional, sacrificing, mutually giving, and encouraging, that enjoys the company of the other without weird attachments or unstated expectations? Is it that we know we're too busy, so we don't even bother? Is it that we fear that any benign form of friendship will eventually be ruined somehow: maybe by gradual, unwelcomed attraction, maybe by distance or drama? Perhaps we don't want to put in the effort. We're more comfortable staying in touch through an occasional text or a thumbs-up on a social media post. Maybe we're afraid to know something different. Maybe we fear being truly known.

That November, the two of us boarded a plane from LA to Houston: a tall white Jewish guy and a short black Christian girl. And we sat around my parents' table in Texas. Mema was there. She explained the whole concept of collard greens to him. I remember him listening intently as she talked about southern cooking and the importance of soul food to the black experience.

Then, to everyone's surprise, he was eager to attend the Bayou Classic with my family: Grambling versus Southern—a football game that is a staple in the tapestry of southern black-college culture.

I remember it was a slightly overcast day when we got to the stadium. He was definitely—as far as my eye could see, anyway—the only white guy there. He stepped down the concrete stadium stairs with confidence and humility, looking as if he had no idea where he was but at the same time reciprocating the huge hug of southern hospitality wrapped around him. He cheered and asked my dad questions about the two teams. He laughed and smiled easily. He leaned in.

Although that Thanksgiving may have been insignificant to him, looking back I now realize just how important it was to me. And I want to do something that we as busy Americans don't stop to do very often or very well: I want to thank him for displaying so beautifully—all those years ago—the way one should enter someone else's home as an invited guest.

I want to thank him for his yes, for wanting to spend a whole holiday immersed in a minority culture, which must have felt like a foreign experience. I want to thank him for taking his privilege and setting it aside to learn, receive, and see life differently, for valuing our friendship enough not just to talk over tacos but also to travel and experience up close what was so near and dear to me.

I want to thank him for listening to my grandmother's words, even though they're faint echoes now, since many of the most precious people in my life never got a chance to hear them firsthand.

I want to thank him for helping me believe that the most unexpected yet fulfilling friendships can help you see what's possible in the realm of relationship—even when the relationship is with someone who is quite literally your opposite.

My friend chose to be in my life and gave me hope that our differences can enrich and deepen us, that what makes no sense on paper or in person can actually lead us to unity and create a different path to togetherness.

I think it's clear that we need a different path.

The path of pure friendship allows us to trust each other's truth and lead each other without requiring that we let go of our own convictions. This path invites us to lift up stories that are different from our own and humbly enter into new experiences. It provides a way for us to listen without feeling fragile or threatened, making time to go the distance, eager to see what's meaningful and true. When friendship is preserved and valued, redemption and healing are possible.

So thank you, my friend. From the quad to my Thanksgiving table, you showed me this different way was viable.

Here's to all the unlikely friendships that have taught us along the way.

19

Chicagoland

(Invitation)

Delicate flakes of snow slid off my brown North Face coat as I shoved my bag over to the passenger seat. The flight from Los Angeles had been long, and I was tired. To make matters worse, this was only my second time in Chicago and the first time that I'd be living in a city with *real* winter—and I was petrified. I'd never driven in snow before, and the walk from the airport terminal to the rental car hub was enough to raise some doubts. I didn't know if I'd be able to make it to my hotel at all.

My face was burning from the wind, my hands numb from the chill. The insides of my nostrils were frozen solid.

I'd decided that this was not, in fact, going to be a good situation.

I gripped the wheel as thoughts of warm and lazy California Sundays tempted me to go back inside and book a ticket west. As the warm air whistled through the heater vents, I thought of the Texas heat and the years when it was warm enough to wear tank tops and eat barbecue out back on Christmas Day.

I might die today, I thought, *but at least I look the part.* I paused to rip my mittens off, deciding that I'd have a better grip on the steering wheel if my palms were slightly sweaty.

I pulled out of the safety of the rental lot, and sheets of snow began pelting my windshield like the neon soap at the car wash. I quickly turned on the wipers and instinctively leaned in close, the tip of my nose just barely grazing the leather wheel.

"Yeah, I'm definitely going to die."

I turned the radio off so I could concentrate. A huge 18-wheeler zoomed past me as I merged onto I-90, headed northwest toward the suburbs.

With graduation behind me, this was how I was starting my new life as an independent adult. I'd accepted a job as a human resources trainee with Nestlé USA and had been transferred to Chicagoland to support one of their facilities. (It was either Chicago, Kentucky—or Iowa. All it took was a quick Google search to determine that as a black twentysomething hoping for a thriving social life, Chicago was my best bet.)

But I'd never lived on my own before, not really. College didn't count. There, I had roommates, resident advisers, and other staff looking after my well-being. I had a schedule to keep and projects to produce. The money for my food came from a plastic card I swiped any time I needed to eat. I had no water or electric or internet bills. There were no calls to plumbers or landscapers or pest control. Now I was beginning life without hand holding or progress reports.

For me, this version of real life began with a snowstorm on a highway in the dead of winter in Chicago.

By some sort of God-ordained miracle, I made it to my hotel in one piece and without passing out at the wheel. I put my gloves back on and gathered my bags, taking a long look at a blue-and-black brush that was lying helplessly on the floor.

"Seriously? Who leaves their *brush* in a rental car?"

I waddled toward the hotel, my unwaterproofed Ugg boots gradually giving way to the mounds of snow and ice.

I checked in and headed up the elevator. Once I got to my room, I pulled back the curtains to look outside. I took off my boots and placed my now-damp socks on the heater to dry. The parking lot lamps were highlighting the raging flurries, giving them their spotlight before they came to their final resting places on car hoods, bushes, and the hotel welcome sign.

I felt my breathing slow, and a deep sigh of relief punctuated the silence.

I made it, I thought.

I pulled out my BlackBerry to call my mom. I knew she'd be wanting to know that I'd made it safely. After one ring, I hopped backward onto the bed, letting my head disappear between the fluffy pillows.

"Hello, darling!" my mom said in her recognizably cheery voice. I could tell by her hurried words that she'd been waiting for my call.

She asked how the flight and the drive were. I lied and told her they were just fine and really easy, no problems.

She asked if I'd checked on the status of my new apartment. I told her it was going to be ready in one to two weeks.

Then she asked if I'd thought about how I was going to make friends.

I paused.

"Well, I was thinking, Ashlee—you know, you could always go to the library or to the grocery store."

"Mom, you can't be serious."

"I am! You love books. And you have to go shopping at some point. Maybe you can meet some people there!"

"Mom, I'm not going to the grocery store to make friends."

As she continued talking, I checked out for a moment to replay her question. Had I thought about making friends? Not really. Even though I wouldn't be caught dead trying to get to know people at a library, she'd touched on an aspect of this new transition that I'd purposefully avoided.

I didn't have any friends in Chicago. I went from having dozens of people who knew and loved me to, overnight, having no one. As I glanced over to the snowstorm outside, I knew that if I didn't want to be completely miserable and isolated, I was going to have to figure something out.

I hung up the phone and sat up straight, realizing how hungry I was. Across from me was the typical black binder with the overpriced room service menu and a list of local stores and services. I flipped through the plastic-reinforced pages, breezing past the eighteen-dollar fruit parfait, and came to a tab in the back labeled "Churches."

If I don't try something, I will *end up attempting to make friends at the sushi fridge,* I thought. *I can see it now: "How's the tempura? . . . Also, where do you hang out on Saturday nights, and can I come?"*

No.

I pulled my laptop out of its case, the keyboard cold to the touch from its trek through the winter tundra.

One by one, I searched every church on the list. One had a website that didn't work. The next congregation was, God bless 'em, all white men in their eighties. The third had a list of core beliefs that made me cringe. The fourth was too far away, and the more I searched, the more weary and hopeless I became. First, I almost died on a freeway. And now it was becoming more possible by the click that I could potentially die of loneliness.

I committed myself to finishing the list. The last church had a working website and a diverse sea of faces. People from different generations and cultures stared back at me with warm smiles and lanyards. I clicked on the "Young Adults" tab and started scrolling through their page. They met together once a month and then in groups around Chicagoland. They were meeting in a specific section at church the next day.

Done, I thought. *It may be the worst experience, but at least I can say I tried.*

The next morning, I bundled up and made my way to my car, only to find that it was completely blanketed in snow. With an audible growl, I yanked open the door and brushed off the snow that had fallen onto the edge of the seat. I started the engine and the wipers and took my mitten off to begin dusting the residual snow off the windshield.

Just then, I caught an older man watching me from his car a couple of spots over.

"Ma'am, do you need a hand?"

"I got it—thank you!" I shouted, the sound muffled by my scarf.

He continued to stare as I swatted the mitten back and forth. It wasn't working. He hung his head with pity and slowly made his way over to me. Approaching the passenger side, he took a look through the window.

"Why aren't you using your brush there?"

I paused. "You mean that's not a hairbrush?"

The man bent over and let out a chuckle, lifting his head to reveal his rosy cheeks. "May I?" he asked.

As I nodded, this man took out the snow scraper and showed me how to scrape the snow and ice off my car properly. He told me to turn the defroster on so it would help melt the ice and to get an automatic starter once my own car had arrived from where it was being shipped.

I thanked the man and made my way to the church. It looked like a college campus or a shopping mall, complete with six different parking lots and a waterfall in the middle of the lobby. I looked up the section number where I knew the young adults would be sitting and made my way there.

Just then, another man stopped me as I looked from the section numbers to the door. He was close to my age, maybe a little older, and if I had to pick one word to describe his appearance, it'd definitely be *jolly*.

"Is this your first time here?" he asked.

"Yes!" I exclaimed. "And I need help. Today's a day that I need a lot of help." Thinking back to earlier that morning, something gave in my spirit.

I thought I was fine—but I wasn't. I was tired and desperate to find people who would want to be my friends. It was helplessly embarrassing to admit, but I was too exhausted to care.

"Well, I need to use the bathroom, but you're welcome to sit with my wife and me!"

———

Looking back at this day—the day when my "real" life started—I realize how different it would've been without two invitations: the invitation to accept help and the invitation to be close.

That day, at some level, I'd come to the end of myself. I was drawn out and away from all that was familiar—to the point that I didn't know a hairbrush from a snow scraper—and had attempted to make my own way. I had tried to use the little I had—in the form of a mitten—to see more clearly, to navigate a massive and unknown place in order to hopefully be found.

But when I'd come to the end of myself, two people saw me—and they stopped. They stopped whatever they were doing to see what was actually happening, and they extended what they had to offer in order to meet me where I was.

Isn't this how we find our way back to one another?

We have to remember what it was like to feel lost and alone, not to know up from down or left from right. We need to recall what it was like being the newcomer in a strange place, the new kid at the lunch table, the new parent at the parents' meeting, the new neighbor or intern or member of the running club.

Our inherent adaptability, which enables us to face the new and the unknown, is also what will help us see the lost and the lonely so we can invite them in.

Do we see people like that now? Do we look for the newcomer, the outcast, or the individual who seems uncertain? Or do we stick to our agendas, taking shortcuts so we won't have to be disturbed or interrupted?

———

The man I met at church that day was named Tyler. His wife's name was Julie. I sat with them on that frigid morning in January, hoping I was doing something right enough to warrant another invitation.

They invited me to their house the following Tuesday, and I met some of the people who would become the most special to me over the next few years. Tuesday is when I met Karen and Ted and Wes and Alexandra. I met Jaci and Jon and Megan and Tracy.

All because one person noticed I was lost and extended an invitation to me.

I didn't need the grocery store or the library after that. And, thankfully, I now know how to use a snow scraper.

But I also know that for the people I meet, an invitation may be all it takes to say *I see you. You're worthy of being seen.*

This world is a big place, and we're all trying to make it, unscathed, from one place to the next. We're all probably more afraid than we seem or more desperate than we look, trying to prove to ourselves and everyone else that we can make it on our own as new grads, new moms, new business owners, new transplants.

But sometimes I think we're all posturing—we're all just waving mittens in the face of what really needs so much more. And sometimes that more is realized only in the effort, risk, and grace of an invitation extended by a complete stranger who just wants to remind us we're not alone.

Whether by the bread section or the biographies or the bathrooms, may we choose to see. Harder yet, may we choose to be seen.

Seeing one another may just be the best way through the storm.

20

Heartbreaker

(Rejection)

Nothing has the potential to challenge one's personal resolve and belief in humanity quite like a good ol' breakup. For decades, romance novels and blockbuster movies have chronicled the dramatic scenes of girls crying on their beds with mounds of tissues strewn about them. There's the classic instant breakup, inspired by an ill-timed return to the apartment, only to find one's significant other shacked up with the sister or the brother or the nanny. There's the breakup conversation that begins "It's not you; it's me" or "I think we should see other people." There's the emotionless jock who's seemingly incapable of expressing his affection, although deep down he's whipped, and the star-crossed lovers who can't catch a break.

But that's what we see on page or screen, a flash of characters' chagrin that usually, one way or another, finds its resolution within fifteen minutes or less.

Real life isn't like that.

Real life may also involve the tissues and the awkward conversations, the puffy eyes or the steady streams of tears. It may feature the bewildered silence between two persons sitting across from each other at a café, wondering if they can still be friends—or, at the very least, acquaintances.

But such scenes are hardly ever resolved in fifteen minutes.

After the last word or final glance back over the shoulder, what lingers is the shame. The embarrassment. The confusion and the replayed words. What lingers is heartbreak.

But heartbreak has a funny way of making us more human. Like a good coach, it leans in, encouraging us to examine all the pieces that are left: our self-esteem, our belief, our worth, and our dignity. It asks us to answer the questions "Who are you?" and "What are you made of?" and "What's next now that this person is no longer occupying that space?"

For some of us, this process takes only a few days. Because of who we are and how we're wired, we can answer those questions in a journal or with a friend and figure out we're better off than before.

For others, the heartbreak throws us into a tailspin, and we ask these questions not out of curiosity but as an existential examination of our deepest selves. We wrestle for weeks and months or even years. We wonder why we're so thrown off balance, frustrated with the fact that we're frustrated.

But eventually, because the passing of time is both mercilessly brutal and tenderly kind, we settle in and accept at least one version of our new post-(insert name here) reality. Once we've wrestled those questions to the mat, one would think that we're done—that we can get a new haircut or move to a new neighborhood or find a new job and start again. The pieces have been reassembled satisfactorily enough to move on.

But the truth is, we're not done.

Heartbreak lays another set of questions before us. Most of us turn away, understandably too interested in our own self-preservation to dig deeper. But the questions patiently persist: "Who is *the other person* to you now?" and "What is he worth?"

In the movies the devastation of heartbreak is cued by dramatic or pop music while one character smashes in her ex's car window with a bat and another burns the heap of clothes belonging to her former significant other. Maybe there's a benign make-out scene that extends for five seconds beyond what's comfortable to watch with your mom, or a photo is ripped to shreds, left to be scattered by one strong gust of wind. But, in large part, we're shown or told that it's okay to hate him—to get revenge and leave him to his demise.

But what if we took a good inventory of all our bad dates and heart-breaks and considered another way?

———

A group of us was sitting around a fire on my friend's cobblestone patio. The sky was a midnight blue, clear enough to look up and see the stars. Others were getting settled, refilling their cups and snack plates as they shuffled between the kitchen and the backyard. It felt good to be together, with friends who knew us and other couples who had been along for the ride of our relationship.

We were on round two. I'd broken up with him one time before, but after sitting together in his backyard on a blanket and looking up at the sun with our hands behind our heads, we decided to try again.

What bothered me so much is that nothing was *wrong* wrong. There hadn't been a blatant foul or a clear breach of trust. There wasn't any disrespect to point to or weird fetishes or hobbies. Something was just— off. Kind of like a door that doesn't quite fit the frame, but you jam it into lock position anyway. Or like a sunken floorboard that you don't bother to fix because you've grown used to the squeaky sound it makes.

That was us. At least, according to me.

Just a few weeks earlier, two of my closest friends had affirmed my unease. They'd sat me down at Panera to tell me that if I were to marry this man, they didn't know if they could invite us to cordial gatherings and holiday parties. And they were dead serious.

Our energies were different: he was an extreme extrovert and I wasn't. Our instincts weren't always aligned. His endearing quirks had become mild annoyances.

But he was incredibly kind and smart and lived life on the edge. He was the definition of adventure.

So we were trying again.

Around the fire, conversation flowed easily back and forth, peppered by occasional bursts of laughter and periods of pin-drop silence as we leaned in and listened to the hard and the good.

At some point, the conversation found its way to us: about our relationship dynamics and our personalities. Most people knew us both fairly well and understood how different we were—but they also understood how we worked. They'd supported us and cheered us on. They'd asked us hard questions and encouraged us to keep going.

But in the middle of what I'm sure he thought to be an innocent description of who I was to him—in detailing the playful way we maneuvered in the kitchen when it was time to cook dinner or clean up—words came out of his mouth that gave him away. They were words heard in the blood-soaked fields of slave masters from the late nineteenth century. They were words of consent and submission muttered by shackled and bound black bodies in an era when saying no wasn't an option. They were words spoken by uneducated yet resilient people. My people. My ancestors.

They were words said aloud in this circle of friends on a starry night in early fall. And as the impact of the words made its way around the circle, my eyes bounced from one person to the next to the next like a pinball, watching as each person lightly gasped or came to a stunned hush.

I stared up silently into the night, knowing heartbreak was coming. There was no question, no third try on the horizon.

With no raised voices or expressed anger, we drove to his house, and the driveway became the dead end.

I left, tears streaming down my face, allowing heartbreak to steep in me freely and wildly. I was embarrassed, knowing that other people had heard his words. It hurt knowing that someone I'd loved could—hopefully unknowingly—speak poison to me.

I got home and became the girl on the bed with the tissues. But I knew I'd made the right decision.

By some miracle, I didn't hate him. I was humiliated and felt foolish, but by grace, I didn't hate him. I continued to see him around after that bad date, the date that ended it all. As strong as my resolve had been, I couldn't *not* still see his kindness, wit, and adventurous spirit. I just knew those good qualities would never be for me to witness up close again.

———

Another scene, this time with a different date.

We'd just come from a holiday party, filled with ugly sweaters and crazy couples' games. He was dropping me off at my car, and though we were separated only by the center console, the space between us felt like solar systems. He stared straight ahead, spaced out and quiet.

"This isn't working."

I didn't understand. "What do you mean?"

Just minutes before, at the gas station, I'd seen a text from his sister— whom I adored—come through on the car's screen. I think he'd told her he was breaking up with me. I think she was just as confused and blind- sided as I was starting to feel in that moment.

More silence.

"This just isn't working."

"Okay, but why?"

Nothing.

After minutes of back and forth that felt like hours, I eventually got out of the car without an explanation and without the person who, just that morning, I would've called my best friend.

More heartbreak. Heartbreak that for months plagued me as I saw him at gatherings and in the halls of our place of worship.

Heartbreak that lingered because there was no neat bow tied at the conclusion to what I'd thought was the biggest gift of my life. I'll never know why we ended. Was it because I was so scattered and disorganized? Was it my depression? Was it because being in an interracial relationship was just too much to handle?

I wrestled the questions about myself down to the ground, and then the one about him looked back at me again, patiently waiting for an answer: Who is he to you now?

This one was harder because the breakup wasn't on my terms.

———

When we don't get to choose the timing or the outcome, it's tempting to become an oppressor. It's tempting to want to inflict pain or at least taint someone's character. It's tempting to metaphorically stand atop another's body, triumphant and unscathed, to make ourselves either the victim or the victor, whichever title paints us in a more favorable light when we tell the tale to friends.

The truth is this: how we handle rejection will ultimately dictate the way we either receive or reject every human we meet from that point forward. It cannot just be about making our own way forward; we have to figure out how to hold other people in our hearts as we move on.

If I'm honest, I'm still confused. Even with a loving husband whom I adore, three kids whom I'm crazy about, and a life rich with meaning and purpose, the confusion still lingers and rears its head.

But I figured something out that has helped me hold sources of bad rejections in good regard: *Even if they weren't able to love me the way I needed to be loved, that doesn't mean they are worthless.*

Their inability to love *me* a specific way doesn't mean they were unable to love at all. It doesn't mean they aren't worthy or good or beloved. Just because they weren't able to love me doesn't mean they deserve my judgment or hate. Just because they couldn't love me doesn't mean they are completely devoid of love.

Even if we experience rejection, that doesn't mean we are rejected. "Accepted" is the only label that's permanent if we're looking to the right Source. But whether it's in a relationship, job, or some other context, rejection can cause us to feel as though our whole selves were wrapped up in someone else's verdict. But that's just the first lie that has to be undone.

The second is that there's only one just way to respond to the one who rejects us. The world will tell us that that way is with vengeance or apathy, with acts of outward or quiet defiance that prove we're not the broken ones.

But vengeance, apathy, and defiance are not quick to leave the heart. They linger and cloud the way we see every enemy and opponent. They build shields of distrust and turn words into fury-filled flames. They tell us that giving grace and being meek are both foolish and weak.

The way we handle rejection, more often than not, tells us much about how we value humanity.

If we choose to reexamine the ways we've handled heartbreak and rejection a little more closely, we can see more than just baseball bats and balled-up tissues. Boyfriends and girlfriends, bosses and teachers, parents and politicians can teach us how to show up holding our own acceptance in one hand and another's worth in the other.

Because, ultimately, real restoration isn't found in the progression of a movie scene or the crease of a page turner. It's found by doing the hard work of rewriting the words rejection has left us with, words about us and about the other person. By transforming words that wound into affirmation, telling the truth about who we are, we also acknowledge the worth of others as they become who they're meant to be outside the confines of relationship with us.

Heartbreak will continue to be part of the human experience. But it doesn't have to pry the dignity out of our humanity.

Regardless of the relational distance or ending or separation, my hope is that we all reach a point where we're committed to the power of forgiveness and the victory of worth over the destructive grenades of vengeance and hate.

My hope is that we find a way forward with our tissues in hand, saying, "No matter what, I know we're both worthy of grasping hold of abundant life."

Even if that life will not be lived together.

21

Unholy Matrimony
(Commitment)

The plastic jar of Vaseline flew across the room and hit the edge of the bedroom window. I whipped around and stormed back into the bathroom, resting my palms on the ledge of the counter. Letting my head drop between my shoulders, I took a deep breath, just then realizing that my arms were trembling in anger.

I was so mad at him. Madder than I'd ever been.

I also knew I'd crossed a line.

The door slowly opened, and he appeared in the frame, scowl fixed firmly between his eyebrows.

To this day, I don't remember what that fight was about. But I remember that the night was long and hard and unbearable.

Whoever told us the first year of marriage would be wedded bliss . . . was lying.

Every moment of rejection and insecurity I'd experienced up until that point felt as if it were boiling over from my heart and out into the air around me. All I was inhaling were gasps of flashbacks filled with fear and shame and embarrassment, all kicked up in a single moment in the heat of an argument with my new and lawfully wedded husband.

Overcome by my emotions, in an attempt to wield control and end the conversation on my terms, I'd picked up a plastic jar of Vaseline—and I'd thrown it. Not at him. But at all the threatening parts of my story that were trying to surface and haunt me again, like a goblin creeping up through a sewer, grabbing at my heels.

The deeper the wound, the harder we fight.

He held the cracked jar in one hand and the broken blue lid in the other. He placed it on the fake marble, gently and without words.

Then he left.

This wasn't the first time. We were only a few months in, and the growing pains were major. He'd been an independent and self-sufficient musician and banker before I met him. I was an independent woman, channeling both my inner Beyoncé and Charlie's Angel, refusing to let any person hinder me from achieving my goals.

Now we lived together, under the same roof and without a clue how to coexist. We both worked at the same church, so there was little space or separation in our lives. The first few months had been hell.

———

Just a few weeks earlier, we'd gotten into an argument and I'd been the one to leave. I'd driven the three blocks to the Fox River and parked my car under a streetlight in the lot by the sorry excuse for a sand volleyball pit. I remember closing my eyes, though the night was already thick with darkness, and asking God to give me words to say to my husband. Every word I'd wanted to say was unloving and disrespectful. Leaving was the best way I knew to create the space I needed. Had I stayed, I would've made things worse.

To him, my departure was abandonment. I hadn't loved him enough to stick around and work things out, even though leaving seemed like the best and healthiest option to me.

We did that to each other a lot in the beginning: misinterpreting signals and making assumptions.

Another time we'd argued on Baptism Sunday. I was standing onstage at church after a beautiful morning of seeing people publicly commit to following Jesus, and he asked me about the Crock-Pot meal I'd assembled that morning. I told him it was chicken—with salsa. He didn't like salsa. I knew he didn't like salsa. But, as I told him from the stage, I'd put it in anyway because "you can't really taste it." And that's where we argued— right there under the shadow of the beams of the wooden cross. Two pastors bickering over poultry by the baptismal pool.

In any other relationship in my life up until that point, I could bail. I could call it quits or not call back or click "No" on the RSVP or break up. I could maintain a safe distance, close enough to benefit from all the good I was determined to see in the people around me, but far enough away not to make a mess. I could play it safe and play nice because I always had the option to leave and never come back.

But Delwin and I were married. Leaving forever would never be an option.

My pride and my pain butted up against his wounds and his routines because day after day we had to say yes to each other again and again.

This is where I learned the true meaning of commitment—in the first six months of our marriage. Commitment wasn't an "I'll be there!" and then a "Hey, something came up. How about next week?" It wasn't me saying I'd leave at seven o'clock, only to be headed out the door thirty minutes later. It wasn't just a feeling or personal resolve or a strong thought or a name on a dotted line. Commitment, I quickly realized, was fiercely active. It was choosing to show up and love him in spite of how I felt. Every. Single. Day.

———

While Delwin was gone, I crawled under the sheets in our bed and cried. First, because I was tired. Second, because I'd thrown a container of petroleum jelly. Third, because how were we *ever* going to be happy like this? And finally, because why was I such a difficult person?

Shame and blame volleyed back and forth, trying to convince me that I should just quit while I was ahead.

In the middle of my dramatic inner soliloquy, I heard the garage door open.

He was back.

He came into the room and sat on the edge of the bed. The tone of the conversation rode the roller coaster of pitch and volume once again, but in the end, he said the words he'd said before: "Ashlee, I just want you to know that—no matter what—I choose you."

As exhausted as we were, he declared that he was choosing me once more. He was choosing the broken and bitter me. He was choosing the depressed and stubborn me. He was choosing the selfish "she was raised as an only child so that explains everything" me.

Something about hearing his words, hearing him choose me *on purpose,* softened my heart, and my rage melted away.

Rejection shapes us and welds our hearts in relationship to the world—but so does commitment. True commitment sees us and says, *I know you, all of you, especially the really deep, dark, and ugly parts— and I pick you and want to do life with you anyway.* It catches all the fear we throw its way. It shelters our stories and creates safe harbors for the times our stories don't make sense. It sits next to us, patiently waiting for us to speak. It tells the truth when it's hardest to hear. And it wades, knee deep, through the depths of the mucky work of real relationship.

———

There were many trips to the river in those first six months. There was even one trip to a girlfriend's house because I knew I didn't want to be alone. I'm not sure where he went when he left, but I'm pretty sure it was somewhere he felt like he could breathe.

But he always came back. I always came back. Because we chose to pick each other anyway. I know there are potentially very few people in our lives who will pick us over and over again—or to whom we'll choose to commit to this depth: our spouses, our kids, our parents, our siblings, a friend or two if we're lucky.

But what if there was a version of this type of commitment that characterized *every* relationship? A commitment that had nothing to do with upholding the holiness of matrimony but everything to do with upholding the holiness of our humanity?

What if we became as inwardly committed to strangers and neighbors and store clerks and the new guy at the golf outing? What if we committed something to the newscaster or the nanny or the cop or the congresswoman?

Our pride and our pain will butt up against others' wounds and routines. When all we want to do is hurl insults across the room or mean tweets across the internet, what would it look like to commit to saying yes to whatever worth we can see and speak to, regardless of the really dark and ugly parts of one another?

We may not agree with another's actions or core values or beliefs, but we can choose at the very minimum to commit to wading knee deep into the muck of dissention and division and discord. We can fight for civility and respect and reverence.

If what we seek for all of humanity is truly worth fighting for, we have to bring all of humanity along with us.

———

Five years later, I still have the broken jar of Vaseline. I keep it as a reminder of two things. First, it reminds me what I'm capable of. It humbles me, lest I believe I'd never resort to knee-jerk reactions in the face of a perceived threat. It gently reminds me to face my pain differently before the hurt wins. Second, it reminds me what commitment looks like. Thankfully, my relationship with my husband didn't end with what was broken. We picked up the pieces, acknowledging what had been shattered in the process. We created some space and came back to look each other in the eye. We chose each other.

In month seven of our marriage, I found out I was pregnant with our first child. This pregnancy came about seventeen months earlier than we'd planned, but her arrival was timely and important. As I cradled her five-pound frame in my arms that Christmas Eve in a hospital bed, I was reminded of how the most wholly beautiful and precious gifts can be born out of commitment's broken offerings. I didn't think we were building much at first, but ten tiny brown fingers and ten tiny brown toes proved otherwise.

A lot has been broken—shattered, even—in places all around us. It's hard enough to commit to those with our own blood flowing through their veins, let alone our communities or those we don't know. But broken plus commitment equals life. And the legacy and hope of new life? That's what's worth fighting for.

22

My Friend, the Republican

(Understanding)

'd just gotten my tonsils removed. They told me that at my age I'd be in a lot of pain. They were right. A week after surgery, the blood vessels in my throat ruptured and I had to go back to the ER for yet another emergency procedure. I arrived home and held my life together with the help of a few essentials: close friends and family, pills and Popsicles.

But the pain of my tonsillectomy paled in comparison to what I felt on the night of November 8, 2016. This pain couldn't be numbed.

I watched from my bed as the results rolled in from the presidential election. A tight knot wrapped itself around my stomach, and the nausea began to rise as the projected outcome became more and more likely.

I found myself unable to breathe normally. Suddenly, I was grateful that I could hardly talk. I didn't have any words to say anyway.

After weeks and months of the presidential campaign, hearing language and seeing headlines that were seemingly pitted against me and others like me—language that degraded women, people of color, immigrants, refugees, and people with disabilities—I was exhausted. My soul was deeply troubled as I wondered, with much anxiety and fear, what this presidency and the rhetoric that accompanied it would mean for the poor, minorities, and marginalized.

Having grown up in Texas, I was in some ways formed by deeply held conservative values surrounding fiscal responsibility and what the church in the South would define as pro-life policy. In Los Angeles I encountered a more liberal approach to social and political values and was encouraged in my more inclusive beliefs around issues like human rights and the protection of the environment. Either way, I'd never felt as if an all-or-nothing approach worked for me politically. So this anxiety wasn't just about the aisle.

As I sat in bed and felt my body reacting to reporters' commentaries and concerned tones, I realized how torn I truly was. Everything seemed wrong. Nothing seemed right. My opinions that had been informed by conservatism didn't feel honored, but neither did the beliefs and values I held that were more aligned with liberal and progressive policies. I was searching for a safe place for my heart to land as the numbers kept rolling in, coming up short. No place felt safe. I was exhausted and felt overwhelmed as I pictured my country's projected future, one ridden with division.

My tears fell freely from my chipmunked cheeks, saturating everything from my hoodie to my yoga pants, and I woke up the next morning unable to tell whether the pounding throb in my temples was from the worn-off Vicodin or my sudden realization that the previous night had not been a dream, as I'd hoped.

My friends, family, and I exchanged a few somber text messages, all of us stunned by this truth: unless we were horribly wrong, we could expect at least four years of wounding words and wild tweets filled with animosity and anger and disdain—from both sides of the aisle.

The intentional and unapologetic stripping away of dignity from the foundations of humankind would continue.

In the days that followed, I knew my default response would be to hide out and start building walls of distrust, creating separation and distance from anyone I felt could look at me, a black woman, with a more emboldened sense of contempt. Suddenly, it was perfectly acceptable—and, seemingly, without consequence—to dip a toe into the waters of racism and bigotry. But the distrust was a two-way street. I was also now hesitant to move freely and be myself. I felt I was constantly asking myself the question, Is there anyone I know who, under the shadow of a ballot box, checked yes—not as a vote *for* a person but as a vote *against* anyone they feel is "other" and therefore unwelcome?

More days passed—minutes feeling like hours—and I knew fear and paranoia were winning. My body was perpetually tense, just waiting for breaking news or the next bout of outrage. My shoulders were tight, my neck was stiff, and my throat hurt, not from stitches but from an ever-present lump that was my body's cue to cry.

Now I found myself wondering what the man at the bar full of white people was thinking of my husband and me when we walked in, or what the woman on the other side of the gas pump could be assuming about who I was. I found myself questioning the motives and intentions of people I went to church with—people who lived across the street or next door.

But in the pockets of silence I squeezed into my day, words I knew all too well—*fear not*—began making their way through the crowd of negative thoughts and hopeless feelings, jumping up and down on tippy toes, trying hard to be seen and acknowledged. And there was a new twist, a small whisper I recognized encouraging me with fresh direction: *fear them not.*

I sensed God encouraging me not just to not fear the newsfeed but also to not fear the people.

At my core, I had to admit I'd been scared of people.

So instead of simply giving way to fear and paranoia, which had already had enough of their way, I decided to take a risk. I reached out to a friend I was 99.9 percent sure had enthusiastically voted for Donald Trump. We'd had passing conversations about the election before, and she proudly wore the Toms shoes with the Republican elephant on them. We couldn't be more different for a variety of reasons, but the relationship we had built over the years was padded with trust and respect. I believe she really loved me, because she'd shown me. I believed she had my best interests at heart, because she'd proven that to be true before.

Even though we were seemingly opposite versions of each other, I trusted that I could take a risk with her. If we're going to keep taking risks for the good of our world and our humanity, they must take place in the safety of trusted relationships, ones that defy the binary structures of our opinions and thought patterns and create a more expansive third way. We'll struggle to be in one another's presence—especially when we're so glaringly different—if we have no interest in maintaining or building relationships based in love, trust, and understanding.

My friend came to my office one day, and I asked her if it would be a good time to throw some potentially hard questions at her. Being one of the least timid humans I know, she was eager to dive in. I closed the door and could feel the tiniest bit of sweat stay put on the metal doorknob as I released it. I was suddenly very warm, and as I sat back down in my swivel chair, I couldn't sit still. I told her how vulnerable I was feeling, but I wasted no more time. "Why'd you vote for him?" I asked, my eyes fixed firmly on hers as I nervously bit the inside of my cheek.

She sat up straight and leaned forward, interlacing her fingers as she rested her elbows on her knees. The expression on her face wasn't fear, but I could tell this was going to be hard for her too. She took a deep breath and told me her truth.

She told me about her heritage and upbringing, which had informed many of her beliefs. Her family's success in business was a strong driver, as was her own legacy of survival. To her, anyone could achieve what her family had, given enough hard work and determination. The policies that supported and protected that legacy were important to her. Donald Trump was her president.

I listened intently as she talked, paying close attention to my emotions as they ran the gamut from anger to tenderness, which bled into happiness and into anger again. We'd had previous conversations when I'd explained to her what it was like to be me: why Black Lives Matter was more than a hashtag to me, why I couldn't use the same shampoo she used, and why I couldn't sass or even casually banter with a police officer if I were pulled over for speeding. We'd talked about how I'd felt about becoming a mom and how she'd felt about the same dream evaporating before her very eyes. We loved the same students. We prayed the same big prayers. We'd committed to the same church family. Yet, as my emotions changed so fast I couldn't keep up, my heart told me to keep looking her in the eye. So I did.

Our conversation ended without raised voices, data, or figures. It ended without me launching into my limited knowledge of white privilege, power dynamics, and their impact on the political landscape. I didn't try to explain why I was so conflicted.

I simply listened. I realized that the hardest work for me wasn't to convince her of anything. The hardest and best work I could do in that moment was to try to understand her, to stand under the weight of her story and to hold it with her, without judgment.

Seeking to understand someone who's lived a different story from ours, collecting different beliefs and values along the way, may be one of the most rebellious and controversial acts we could choose in our current cultural landscape.

Everything in us wants to push back and prove we're right, to shout the truth according to our politics, to comment and retweet and post and poke until the offenders—whether "those" left-wing Democrats or "those" right-wing Republicans—understand just how wrong and stupid they really are.

Politics aside, have we lost our ability to submit to another's story? To yield to someone else's perspective, even if only temporarily, to try to honor an experience that we didn't live? To surrender our urgency and our expertise and hear a perspective that we've perhaps never cared to welcome? My guess is this is harder for those who've benefited from power and privilege than it'd be for someone on the fringes and the margins. It's hard to let go of that which has proven to be successful and beneficial. It's even harder to move from hearing to making different choices in our lives that ensure others' lives are as valued as ours. That type of resolve takes deep humility.

We won't find our way back to mutual respect and love for humanity through harsh judgment and rhetoric. Because the office of ultimate judgment was never assigned to us to begin with.

━━━━

Two years after the election, I sat in my friend's home. I held her new baby girl, bouncing her as I walked around the living room, trying to give my friend a break.

I don't know what she thinks of the president now, nor have I asked. But I have shown up for her, trusting in both the history of our relationship and a power beyond my own that my presence in her life—and hers in mine—is probably one of the most holy and effective agents for both of us in how we see the rest of the world. From me, she gets a different perspective on day-to-day life in America. I don't hold back or sugarcoat my reality for her, but I tell my stories in a way that help her see. From her, I get a different perspective on what it means to have built something and then feel as if it might be taken away, a narrative I believe is as old as time but for her is present and hers to protect.

She's taught me the power in mutual understanding, how crucial it is to carry that into our well-established friendships and into interfaces with complete strangers or enemies.

There's always, always more to the story.

The pain from the election still lingers when I see 280 characters in all caps or reports of the death of a child who was under government custody. We're called to take action, to actively work for justice and peace. We're not to sit back and spectate and hope someone else will lead.

But we are not to operate within the limiting and deceiving boundaries of categories we've created. We are not to fear people or fight them along the way. Each soul is holding a story that we'll never know unless we see the value in drawing near, asking questions, and listening. Maybe the invitation will be declined, but at least our hearts will be expanded, strengthened in new ways, not just by the fullness of the work of righting wrongs but by the rebellious and controversial work of seeking to understand those we've deemed unworthy.

The stories we tell ourselves over and over again, whether they're about a person or a group of people, are the most dangerous when we replay them outside the context of personal relationship. And the only way we're going to end the cycle of fear-based discord is by pulling ourselves back into relationship, replacing the dangerous stories with what's real: real humans, real hearts, real connection.

23

The Big Chop

(Loss)

O nce he started, I couldn't go back. The buzz of the clippers was the only sound I could hear as I felt the weight of one, then two, clumps of hair fall to the cold tile floor.

"Are you okay?" he asked.

"Mmm hmm," I muttered shakily, my voice barely audible under the dominance of the metal teeth.

He continued around the back and edges of my neck, working his way up until he got to my crown.

"I think I'll leave this part a little longer than the rest—just until it grows out a little more."

"Okay," I squeaked in the same hushed voice.

I was terrified, but I knew the hair had to go.

━━━

When I was a little girl of four, five, six, my hair reached down to my waist. It had never been tainted by chemicals of any kind, having been handled only by my mother's greasy and efficient hands and my grandmother's long and delicate fingers wrapped around the wooden base of a hot comb. Every week, my mother would take Blue Magic Conditioner Hair Dress or Luster's Pink Lotion and run its brightly colored contents along the tracks of my scalp, massaging my head with her rounded fingernails and lulling me to sleep. She'd wipe her hands on an old dish towel between sections and then ready herself for the task of putting eight to ten plaits or twists in my hair with the little clear plastic barrettes at the end.

When we were going out for a fancy occasion—*The Nutcracker* at the Houston Ballet or the mother-daughter luncheon hosted by my school—she'd brush it straight, and like chocolate-colored cotton candy, it would lightly float and bounce off the back of my shoulders, tickling my ears and leaving a shine on the back of my neck.

Sometimes, when I was at Mema's house in Mexia, Mema would fire up her stove and place her metal combs on top of a burner until they were scalding hot to the touch. Then, after sectioning the wild city that was my head of hair into neatly boxed neighborhoods, she'd carefully straighten the sections, and my hair would keep going and going until I couldn't even feel where the strands ended. Those days in the Texas heat were unbearable. Sweat would drip from both of our brows, but I was so proud of how much hair could grow from my head.

Then it wasn't good enough for me.

I remember sitting in front of the television in our family room at home, watching light-skinned women swing their hair back and forth, waving it through the air like a banner of beauty.

I couldn't do that with my hair.

So I started asking my mother to allow me to chemically straighten it.

"No, Ashlee," she said. "Once you start straightening it that way, it'll lose its strength and may break over time."

I didn't care. I wanted straight hair I could throw into a messy bun or a ponytail like all of the other girls—white, Indian, Nicaraguan, Mexican—at my school.

I wanted hair that could be braided in the lounge and curled with a CHI iron.

I wanted hair that I could run my fingers through without catching them in black kinks and knots.

One day my mother finally gave in. I could tell she was tired too of all that hair, as well as the hours it took to do it herself. She was a full-time professional who worked hard at home and in the marketplace. I think that first appointment was an admission that, no, she couldn't do it alone.

So I sat in the salon chair that very first time when I was nine years old. I smelled the burn of the chemicals rising from the black bowl. The stylist, wearing white latex gloves, painted my roots with the white magic, leaning over and asking me every once in a while if my scalp was burning. It stung a little bit, but I knew it'd be worth it.

At the end of two and a half hours, my hair was silky and straight and shiny and—*perfect*. From then on, every six weeks the white magic would make my hair straight again, from elementary to high school through college; from Houston to Los Angeles to Chicago. From stylist to stylist I endured the changes and transformations that naturally accompany the progress of life. Yet one thing remained: my hair, bone straight, starved of is natural curl and coil. Starved of its freedom.

Eventually I had my first two kids, and as my body changed, so did my hair. It grew weak and started to break. My scalp was reacting to treatments like never before. I couldn't keep the ends healthy.

A few weeks after the election, we flew down to Houston to spend Thanksgiving with my family.

It was my first time seeing Mema in a new place that wasn't her home out in the country. She was living in a hospital bed in an eight-room home that had been transformed into an assisted living facility. Her speech was mostly incomprehensible. Her eyes stayed closed the majority of the time.

I held her cold hands, her bones covered only by a thin veil of veined skin. Leaving there, where other women were waiting for their families to visit, waiting for dinner . . . or death, I realized that I'd been chasing after someone else's idea of authenticity and value.

I buckled myself into the passenger's seat next to my mom and looked in the rearview mirror. Sitting behind me was my almost-two-year-old daughter, resting her head on the side of her car seat, her two Afro puffs crowning her head with curly, kinky little-girl glory.

I knew then that I wanted—no, *needed*—to start over.

As my hairstylist put the finishing touches on my hair, I swallowed hard and glanced down at his feet. Mounds of black strands lay there, lifeless. Years of comparison and self-loathing had fallen from my head. Seasons of trying to look glamorous and nonexotic and mainstream were severed from my story—and now all I had to offer was 100 percent me. There was no one else to hide behind.

I left the salon and knew my mother would be devastated. She'd never wanted me to cut my hair, even considering the potential consequences of a chemical relaxer. It'd taken so long for it to grow. I knew if Mema had eyesight good enough to see, she'd be crushed too.

I imagined they might feel their years of hard work and tender care were now gone, replaced by space and only short strands of growth and life.

But what they would potentially see as loss, I saw as gain.

I saw a fresh start, a new leaf, a statement of acceptance and self-worth. I saw legacy, an example to my daughter that she could wear straight hair if she wanted to—but that she didn't have to in order to be beautiful. I saw a chance to refocus my life on what really mattered to me, no longer distracted by the chokehold of comparison.

With my short hair—with the loss of what once was—I was free.

I visited Mema again the next day, just a couple of days after Thanksgiving. It would be the last time I'd see her, just the two of us. I sang "Amazing Grace" and held her Dasani water bottle, gently tipping it, guiding the cool liquid toward the back of her throat. I stroked the back of her hand and wiped her face with her towel, tucking her in and praying over her.

She saw me free.

She saw me unhindered by years' worth of unkindness to myself. Now I could love her with the fullness of everything I was and everything I had.

Mema passed away just thirteen days after our last visit. Another loss. This time, I didn't feel so free. I felt the burden of grief sitting on my chest, crushing me, making me feel immovable and small.

I wanted her back. I wanted her voice, her laugh, her fingers in my hair. I wanted her smile, her confident and quick walk, her wisdom, her peace, and her prayers.

One loss on the tails of another. One welcomed and freeing, one weighty and throwing me into a frenzy of nothingness. For days I couldn't tell which way was up or what way was forward.

In both situations I couldn't go back. Both losses left me changed, a more authentically available and human version of myself. Because I had to feel both the freedom and the grief, I was now more sensitive to the impact of loss in others' lives. I wasn't always available to it, too consumed with my own loss, but I recognized it. And I knew it was forming or transforming something in the others, changing their worldview or the way they loved.

We often don't like celebrating or revisiting our losses, which can haunt us. But taking a closer look at the chasm of loss can also potentially heal us.

Loss can show us the places where we've truly become free; it can mark the legacies of the people and moments that have given us the greatest gifts. We're transformed by loss, whether or not we choose it.

The loss of my hair was the beginning of a new day, a new season of acceptance of the woman I knew God had created me to be.

The loss of my grandmother was the beginning of a long season of reflection, a new journey of noticing and remembering how much she'd truly meant to me and the difference she'd made in my life.

Although we cannot choose the inevitability of the transformation, what we can choose is to allow loss to do its work in helping us see others who are healing or hurting, those who are newly found and freshly scarred. It can make us more human and transform those who would otherwise be invisible to us into humans too.

———

Two years after my big chop, I was sitting in bed and instinctively reached up to play with my new and wildly growing strands of black and brown hair. This was hair untouched by the threat of unnatural product or my low self-esteem.

It was just after Christmas, the season when I think of Mema most.

I remembered the handful of friends and strangers who had asked me about my hair and why I'd cut it off. I remembered the sense of peace and pride I felt as I explained my reason—that it was a symbol of a deeper transformation—and how many of those people seemed to respect, but not understand, my decision.

I remembered the friends and strangers who'd lost loved ones over those two years and how I could, with absolute truth and empathy, tell them that I also knew the sting of loss. More times than not, they were there to comfort me when the grief crept back and stung afresh. Who knew that loss could do that? That it could clear the way and leave the space for us to grow into more of ourselves, in deeper empathy for one another.

24

Shabbat

(Silence)

The tour bus was abuzz with excited chatter as we approached the apartment in Jerusalem. The twenty-two of us were intoxicated with a cocktail of fatigue and reverence as we anticipated our next stop.

We were midway through our ten-day journey. My luggage had been lost somewhere between New Jersey and Tel Aviv, and I looked like a vagabond who had been traveling for a month: dusty and basic with a greasy sheen on the surface of my skin. My jeans were starting to smell like old air. My plain gray sweatshirt told everyone who saw me that I cared very, very little about anything except my travel comfort.

All the other women looked fresh with their washed faces and perfumed wrists, ready to receive the offering of this Holocaust survivor and her husband.

Regardless of what we looked or smelled or sounded like as the bus let out its final hiss upon arrival, it was safe to say that our hearts were sober.

My expectancy was tainted by the horror and heavy weight of one of our first stops at Yad Vashem, the Holocaust museum and memorial in Jerusalem. I'd walked the outdoor pathways and read the stories of men and women who'd perished and persevered. I'd slowly spun around in the Hall of Names, its innermost cone memorializing those who'd perished. Its walls were lined with black books containing names and stories of those whose faces we couldn't see but whose lives we knew were worthy. At the entrance to the hall, these words were etched in stone:

> I shall give them in My house and within My walls a memorial and a name. (Isaiah 56:5)

It was the beginning of the Sabbath, the day of rest—called Shabbat in Hebrew. We'd prayed alongside other women at the Western Wall, the holiest site according to Jewish tradition, passing by young soldiers with rifles on their backs, rabbis, and mothers with children. Although men and women were divided on either side of a partition, unity was thick as the joy of the Sabbath and the final rays of the setting sun settled among the people.

Now we were going to be the guests of a woman who'd been denied hospitality for so long.

We filed off the bus one by one and then headed up the concrete steps of a narrow stairway.

The sky was still pink and yellow over the city, not yet ready to let go of daylight's brightness.

After making our way up the stairs, we were welcomed into a spacious yet cluttered apartment. She greeted each of us with a smile, pulling us in as if to express her own sense of urgency and excitement.

We were strangers. Yet we were her guests.

The same buzz that had filled the bus now tucked itself into the corners of her house. We took our seats around a table ready to feed thirty, since she and her husband had invited neighbors over to help host us.

Her husband stayed put at the head of the table, his limited mobility clear by the way he slumped in his seat. Yet his expression energized me.

We grabbed our plates and filled them with the treats of Shabbat, forming a single-file queue from the tiny kitchen to the back of the living room as we shuffled slowly past precious photos that told the stories of their lives together. Our hostess stood by her husband's side as she directed us to a little booklet that she'd placed at each setting.

She lit candles and prayed the kiddush blessing over the wine. She then prayed over the challah bread before it made its journey around the table. The seemingly somber introduction to the meal was then broken by songs of joy and gratitude. Our group joined in with our weak voices, but we knew the strength of this display of solidarity. We were welcomed and we were one.

After the meal and the laughter and the sharing of stories and small talk with table neighbors, our hostess once again took her place next to her husband.

This time, it was our turn to consume a different offering. She began to share her story.

She told us of her childhood and showed us black-and-white photos of her in dresses and hats from a large book.

Then she told us how she escaped the horror of the beginning of the Holocaust. All I can remember is that she ran. She ran for her life, never to see her family again.

The shadow of her trauma and sadness spread from my end of the table, where I sat only one person away, all the way down the lace table-cloth past empty plates and elaborate dishes to the dark end of the room. Hushed silence, punctuated only by an occasional cleared throat, was the new soundtrack of the now-shaded dinner table, the yellow and pink of the sky long gone and replaced by midnight blue.

She let the silence do its work, allowing the echo of her story and her survival to wash over us, cycling through our heads and hearts. I remember being paralyzed by her pain, yet somehow I felt as if I were not worthy of hearing her story. She had laid her heart wide open before us, right next to the crumbs of challah.

Then she turned the attention on us.

"Let's go around the table," she said, with surprising cheer in her voice. "I want to know about the most impactful part of your trip so far. What have you enjoyed the most about Israel?"

She spoke with confidence in her voice, clearly proud of her country. One by one, we took turns around the table, sharing how we'd enjoyed Jerusalem, the food, and the people. A couple of people dared to tell her that we'd stayed in Palestine, a place she never acknowledged containing people who, to her, were not worthy of mentioning.

"You stayed in Bethlehem?" she asked, her eyes squinting. Her eyebrows crept closer together. I sensed a hint of suspicion.

We had stayed in Bethlehem. We'd dined in Palestinian shops and had given our money to Palestinian merchants. Not only that but we'd sat at the feet of Palestinian women and heard their stories—stories that differed from the ones I'd seen represented in black and white in local newspapers.

For some reason, my stomach began to churn as my turn approached. I was fully aware, as I always was, that I was the only person of color at that table, a minority in a sea of majority hues, even though we were miles from home.

To my left, our guide took his turn. His voice seemed muffled, since all I could hear was my own breath rising and then hiding in my chest, as if to say *Courage, fear, courage, fear.* In and out, until he trailed off and then looked my way.

"Well," I started, "I've really enjoyed the hospitality that's been shown to us by everyone: Palestinians, Israelis, everyone."

There was a long pause. I looked directly into her face and was met with a full-on scowl. The smile she'd worn earlier had become a tight-lipped line. Without breaking her gaze, she launched into questions, which she hadn't asked the other twenty-eight people.

"Where'd you go to school?" she asked.

I told her I'd attended USC in Los Angeles.

"Interesting," she said, dryly.

She told me that someone in her family had attended Stanford and that Condoleezza Rice had visited there once.

"You know," she continued, "I wonder—is interracial marriage widely accepted in the States? It's not so much here." She looked at me and then to our guide next to me. Had she assumed we were a couple?

More silence.

"Yes, it's more widely accepted and even celebrated in some cases. Although there are some parts of the country where it's still frowned upon." I looked up to see who'd spoken. It was my friend. She was sitting directly across from me, and she looked at me with determination as she spoke.

More silence.

The Holocaust survivor continued. "I'm really looking forward to your president's arrival here in a few weeks," she said, still looking my direction. "I think the relationship between our two countries will be helpful, don't you think?" Her stare lingered a little longer. After a few painful seconds, she shifted her gaze slightly to the last member of our group, a woman whose life work was mostly based in Palestine.

I could feel that familiar lump in my throat as I forced back tears. I felt as though I were still the center of attention, and although the conversation had moved on, the tension and hostility were still clinging to me. I remember feeling as if I wanted to disappear underneath the table, through the floor, never to be seen again.

I was seven years old again. *"Do you shower?"*

I was in the senior lounge again. *"You know you only got in because you're black."*

I was in Jamba Juice again. *"Nigger!"*

By the time the last guest had finished, it was clear we had overstayed our welcome. Our hostess encouraged us to help clean up. We all stood, quickly, and took our plates to the sink. Then, one by one, she took our hands and led us out her door. She didn't even look at me. Taking my hand, she all but pushed me out into the stairwell.

Our dinner was over.

On the ride back to our hotel, the bus was now abuzz with a different sound. Some women were frustrated that we'd chosen to mention the full breadth of our travels to our gracious hostess. Others were furious on my behalf, speaking up for me, experiencing—perhaps for the first time—the exhaustion of needing to manage the presence of outright hostility that I've always faced because of my black body.

The tension rose as we entered our hotel lobby, where we gathered in a nearby sitting area to process aloud.

Women spoke, going back and forth, defending and speaking their opinions. Some were silent, observing from their corners. The joy and unity that had marked us just hours before was seemingly unraveling at the seams.

Finally, I spoke.

"Ladies, thank you for speaking up for me. But I don't need you to. I can speak for myself. What we experienced is something I'm not a stranger to. My whole life, I've had to hold honor and respect in one hand and anger and sadness in the other—just to survive."

I wasn't mad at this woman, this survivor who'd endured her own hell and made it out alive. But I was deeply saddened. I was weary from the weight of the reality that you can be a survivor yet still hold hate by the hand.

I went to bed that night limp and zapped of life. We still had travels ahead of us, where I'd need to lean in and listen some more. Experiences that would require me to bite my tongue and consider a different way. I would need to sit silently yet again, suspending my own feelings and emotions and truth in order to make space for the feelings and emotions and truth of another.

In the pursuit of peace and true unity, silence is oftentimes so much more difficult to hold than our own spoken truth.

That night, I received both hospitality and hostility. I was the recipient of both strength and suppressed aggression. *Both. And.* All woven together with the threads of silence.

In the work of seeing the image of the Creator in the person sitting across the table, it's tempting to want only the hospitality and the strength. We want only what feels good, what benefits our side and our story.

But the most important work can be birthed from the place where uncomfortable silence seeps between us. In those moments we're faced with the decision of whether to respond immediately with the assuredness of our truth or to let the silence work in us. To feel the sadness and anger and grief. To be reminded that there's more at work in the story of the other and that perhaps true peace requires the sacrifice of our own beloved stances in the pursuit of greater justice.

What is won when the silence is broken? When we combat our opponents with hurried incredulity?

I still believe our hostess did not fully accept me. But on the off chance we meet again, my silence and restraint hopefully made a way for us to tell more stories—for her to hear more about what makes me worthy and for me to hear about her hopes for the future she never thought she'd see.

All was not lost. When we let silence do its work, we leave space for the delayed hope of possibility. We may not have spoken our piece, but we leave space for the peace that could one day break through and draw us closer in our humanity.

Shabbat. Rest. Pause. There truly is joy and hope in the Sabbath.

25

Black Power

(Context)

N o one was talking. As I scanned the room, looking at each face, no eyes met mine except for my two coleaders'. One looked back at me with a twitch in the crease of her mouth, her eyebrows positioned in the middle of her forehead as if preparing to make room for our students' big and confusing feelings.

I let the silence linger a little longer, allowing the polite buzz of the overhead lights to be the only active participants in our debrief. The tiled floor was cool enough to feel beneath the one sock I had rested on the floor, which felt nice given the warmth of the room. I tucked my other foot beneath me and shifted my weight, my elbow on the worn couch, my fingers resting on the side of my temple. I tried to mute my sigh as my chest rose and fell. I knew they needed more space to think. It wasn't time to break the silence just yet.

This dormitory in Alajuelita, Costa Rica, had been home to our team for the past six days. The sixteen high school students had started the week with excitement and expectation, eager to make new friends and support the church we'd come to serve. In the beginning, strangers quickly became friends over fidget spinners and Snapchat stories shared at departure gates and in airplane aisles. Camaraderie formed over concrete mixing and metal-beam spraying and hole digging as we worked mornings at the church. Hearts were joined as we worshipped in a language that most of us didn't know well and ate lunch under the blue tent as Vilma and other church mothers taught me how to make empanadas in the little concrete kitchen next to the church entrance.

Despite not knowing the language, we communicated with the locals using our eyes and facial expressions. Every afternoon it had worked out, somehow. Hot lunches made their way into our hungry bellies. Although we were all dripping in paint and sweat, I knew we were welcomed and loved by people who, just a few days earlier, had been altogether unknown to us.

The days had been long, but they'd filled me. Each afternoon we returned to the dormitory in a quiet neighborhood just a few minutes from the church and headed up the stairs to rest in our rooms. The dormitory looked like a small hospital, with lots of tile floors and close-set windows and doors. In the center of the lobby was a courtyard filled with plants, grounding our temporary home in the tropical beauty for which the country is known. In the rooms around and above this courtyard, we'd slept and processed and journaled and rested.

But this day had been different.

This day, new friends had taken us down the street and off a beaten path, up and around homes tucked into tiny crevices, many stacked so close together that what we thought were adjoining rooms were actually separate residences. Pastor Richard, the young shepherd of this church who had come to our work site every day after his full-time job to encourage and cheer us on, led us with a smile permanently plastered to his face. He walked quickly and with intention, clearly not fazed by the labyrinthine neighborhood. This was the community he served. He led us over hard, hot ground, single file, up slopes and down rocky streets that were void of any sign or plaque to identify where we were. Beto, the stray dog that had forced his way into our hearts by hanging out with us at the church during our construction days, followed us, swerving from the left of one person's heel to the right of another's, his light brown legs quickening to keep up.

We'd rounded a corner and then, without warning, the nineteen of us were facing a clearing of flattened soil and a handful of tall trees surrounded by homes. But these homes were not made of brick and siding and stone as ours were back home. These homes were made of sheet metal, the floors compacted dirt.

Pastor Richard, with his wide smile and charisma, shook hands with one of the residents. Then, as if the community had been expecting our arrival, groups of kids and their families came out of their homes to meet us. Without any formal introduction, kids initiated games of tag with our students, some of whom seemed to still be in shock from what they were seeing. I looked one way and saw a boy hoisted on the shoulders of one of our students. I looked the other and saw another student who spoke Spanish talking to a mom.

A few minutes later, I found myself being welcomed through the doorway of one home. My feet met dirt as the homeowner proudly showed me where she did laundry and where her baby slept. I turned around once and the tour was done. As we headed back outside, I saw one student's face red with the evidence of freshly wiped tears. She smiled through her shock as we picked up a couple more students and headed to another family's home, this one with floors. They told us their story, which we were able to understand with the help of an interpreter: the mother had given her husband a kidney and had then carried her now five-year-old son to full term despite the risk to her pregnancy. We sat squished together on one of their couches, opposite her and her husband, and listened and nodded. No words, just bodies being present, hoping to communicate honor and respect for her hospitality and the lives she and her family had lived.

Now here we all were, sitting around the lounge of this dormitory, silent once again. One student had never been on an airplane before this trip. A handful of them had been exposed only to the wealth and privilege of their schools and neighborhoods. I knew that much still had to sink in. Just by looking at their faces, I could see that the collective internal wrestling was loud and boisterous—an arena of noise trying to reconcile the comfort of their personal lives with the sights of extreme poverty.

The silence was broken when a stranger opened the lounge door. "Excuse me?" he said.

He spoke in Spanish, and all nineteen of us instinctively looked at the one student we knew could understand him.

"He wants us to turn off the lights," she said, matter-of-factly.

I looked at him and said in English, "We're going to bed soon, sir."

He said something else, this time with extra sternness, and then shut the door, disappearing into the dark hallway.

"How'd he get in here?" I asked with a smile.

There was a collective giggle as we all realized that a man we didn't know had somehow just made his way into our dormitory unnoticed—breaching premises we had thought were secure. He was an innocent neighbor who'd been disturbed by our light being on past ten o'clock at night, but still . . .

I was secretly thankful for his interruption. Stranger or not, he'd broken the silence.

From that point on, student after student shared her shock and guilt and gratitude—some through tears. As they processed aloud, I could tell that what they'd thought to be true about their worldviews and vantage points now was shifting. Their discomfort came in confronting new people up close rather than through the distance of billboard ads. Instead of begging for a few cents, as some students had expected from selective television programming, our new brothers and sisters had been full of joy, dignity, and confidence. They had welcomed us into their homes with excitement. They'd given more to us than we had given to them. They'd made us the recipients, the beneficiaries, the ones coming in with empty hands and leaving with full, conflicted, expanded hearts.

We processed what the day had changed or affirmed. I reminded the students that our wrestling wouldn't end that evening, that it would be healthy if it continued into the last few days of our trip.

The best growth happens in the wrestling. When we think of a newborn child entering the world or the first blades of grass pushing through the soil each spring, we realize that struggle has the power to change us in ways that stagnancy never could. Done with intentionality and care, such grappling yields life. It yields growth and gives a new texture to everything we knew before. This is what I was hoping for my students, that their wrestling would not be in vain but that because of their openness to a new context that challenged their own, their lives and their understanding of God and the kingdom would be enriched.

———

The next day, we headed back to the church for a final day of fun with our new friends. They'd set up a soapy slide on a large blue tarp, and it was just what we needed to exhale from the previous day. Our students and other teenagers from the neighborhood took turns sliding down the tarp, trying their best to avoid the jagged rocks that were poking up through the ground.

Then it was time for a friendly game of soccer.

"Ashlee, come play!" Pastor Richard shouted across the grass. I'd been huddled under the overhang of the church, tossing a Frisbee with a few young kids.

With a lot of persuasion from my students, I finally gave in. I'd eaten way too many empanadas and cups of *arroz con leche* that week and hadn't played soccer since I was nine years old. But I wanted Pastor Richard to know that I was committed to the cause.

He'd changed from his work clothes into his soccer gear, ready for serious competition. His short, curly black hair bounced up and down as he ran to his post, his tan skin standing out as darker than the other Ticos (a nickname Costa Ricans affectionately call themselves). His build was more reminiscent of an American football player's, but he was quick and nimble, his feet dribbling the ball through the field that was accented with mud puddles from a previous rain.

The game started, and his signature smile was gone, replaced instead by a stern athletic focus.

I was in trouble.

I hung to the side and to the back, exerting only enough energy to kick the ball away from my team's goal a couple of times.

I pretended to move around without doing anything effective. Honestly, my main concern was that I wasn't wearing shin guards, so I imagine I looked more like a foosball player gliding back and forth without a ball than I did a World Cup hopeful. Then, without intending to, I found myself on offense, challenging Pastor Richard in an attempt to make my way to the goal. I did an awkward shuffle move in my shoes—now destroyed by the mud—knowing I would likely have only one chance to get in a good kick. I saw my teammate in my periphery, waiting for his chance to score.

By some miracle of that accidental fancy footwork, I maneuvered the ball around Pastor Richard and directed the ball toward my teammate.

Apparently, the move was too good.

Pastor Richard tripped and fell to the ground. The watching crowd of students and neighbors instinctively let out a chorus of "Oooooh!" and chuckles as everyone reacted to the only legitimate soccer move I'd ever pulled off in my life.

Richard sprang back up, his shirt covered in mud, his smile reappearing as he held my shoulders and looked me in the eye. His eyes widened, and he was beaming.

"BLACK POWER!" he shouted, raising his hand for a high five.

A sudden hush settled over the field. The activity on the soapy slide seemed to come to a complete halt. The students who were playing with kids on the other side of the field by the church looked over toward Richard. If there'd been music playing on a record, it would've come to an abrupt scratchy stop.

No one moved.

I looked around, checking for my students' responses. I was smiling, but I could tell my students—none of whom were black—were conflicted. This time, they were wrestling for a completely different reason. Their expressions quickly shifted from amused to horrified.

I looked at Richard and paused.

Then I awkwardly raised my hand to meet his. "BLACK POWER!" I yelled for the entire field to hear.

He and I laughed at the absurdity of the rally cry.

Everyone around us looked confused. I think most were expecting me to be offended, insulted by the casual use of a phrase that packs such a meaningful and pointed racial punch back in America.

But in that moment, I knew something they didn't know. I knew that Pastor Richard and I were sharing something that joined us together despite our different contexts. The people we served were vastly different. The churches where we worked were different sizes with opposite financial realities. Our languages were different, as were our family backgrounds.

But I knew that because of his skin color, in Costa Rica he was considered black. His dark skin made him stand out—as did mine. After our trip I learned that there was more at stake than just standing out. I read about the complicated history of racism in Costa Rica, learning that descendants of black railroad workers had been intentionally discriminated against because of the color of their skin.[9]

Although Pastor Richard and I didn't get a chance to share our experiences of race in detail, it was one of a handful of things we had in common. Even though he was a Tico pastor from Costa Rica and I was a black church worker from America, and his community was trying to survive and meet basic needs while members of my community were more concerned with getting into good schools so they could get well-paying jobs, we'd found something that united us.

Even if it was the source of a lot of tension and potential pain. Even if it was a little taboo to shout it across the field in a sea of people with light skin.

We'd found something.

That day, Pastor Richard celebrated my blackness the best way he knew how, while also acknowledging his own.

The day before, my team of students and I had celebrated others' hospitality and kindness the best way we'd known how, while also acknowledging the vastly different context of our lives.

Silence had created the space necessary for us to wrestle and observe and shift and see.

And isn't this the beauty of entering contexts that are different from ours? We get to hold up our experience against that of another, allowing both celebration and struggle to mark and mold us, while acknowledging the beautiful and the broken, the familiar and the foreign.

But the key is, we have to acknowledge *all* of it.

In recognizing the context of our lives, we can be honest about our realities, while being expanded by the experience of another. It doesn't have to be either, one, or none. We can feel both gratitude for our lives and sorrow for how poverty runs rampant. We can be shocked by what someone said and also appreciate that their words could actually be steeped in rich meaning that helps us better understand our role and responsibility to them and to humanity.

The silence was broken when Richard and I embraced. By holding both our contexts together, we gave permission and freedom to those watching. All was well.

I wonder how different our conversations would be if we were more sensitive to context. If we asked questions about how a person might be experiencing us versus how we experience them. It's so easy to jump to conclusions or get defensive, not allowing the work of context to enrich and shape what we already know. Making room for context doesn't make us weak or inferior; it stretches us and invites us to push through the tension of fear, doubt, shame, or guilt to experience positive growth as we come to understand the life of another person. But we must acknowledge that both the fear *and* the hope exist. That both the guilt *and* the humility are present. That both the history *and* the future are important. Wrestling without the referee of context, without acknowledging all that's there and true, isn't enriching at all. If we don't recognize context, we create room for shame and guilt, for hurt and misunderstanding. Embracing context helps pave the way for growth.

Growth means seeing that those who have less might actually be richer in hospitality and grace and Christlikeness.

Those who speak a different language might actually be able to identify with a part of our struggle.

Those who live in a different neighborhood or work in a different department might actually be able to teach us something about ourselves.

But we have to decide whether to let context do its work of expansion and growth, whether we'll allow context to take hold and lead us.

Each one of us has this kind of influence—to bring what we know to the lounge or the field and let someone else teach us, wrestling well as we lean in and listen. When we do, we'll see that power isn't reserved for the elite few. The power to enrich and expand your life and mine belongs to all people.

26

Protests and Police

(Risk)

Scrolling through Facebook and Instagram in the wake of the rally and protests in Charlottesville in August 2017 was enough to make my stomach churn.

> The rally on Saturday was organized in opposition to a plan by local officials to remove a statue of Robert E. Lee, the Confederacy's top general, from Emancipation Park in Charlottesville. That plan prompted a similar protest in May, led by the white nationalist Richard B. Spencer, as well as a Ku Klux Klan rally in July. . . . However, the forces behind the rally run much deeper than the removal of statues. Right-wing extremism, including white nationalism and white supremacy, is on the rise, according to the Southern Poverty Law Center. And a string of killings in recent months raised the specter of far-right violence well before last weekend.[10]

I wasn't hungry. I couldn't sleep. All I could see when I closed my eyes was a soft orange glow reflecting on white faces filled with rage. I couldn't tell if the images were from the civil rights movement or now. I couldn't tell if these people were strangers, friends, nobodies, or high school acquaintances. It was all a blur. Yet as I rocked my seventeen-month-old son and rubbed lotion into my baby girl's chocolate skin, the blurred images sharpened into focus and I realized just how thick the fear really was.

A friend texted me to ask if she could come over. She must've known how I was feeling. She came over with her two sons and occupied space with me that I temporarily had no idea how to fill.

I remember showing up to work the Tuesday after the rally and looking at everyone with a different filter, wondering, *Did you think it was just as awful as I did? Did you say anything? Did you lose sleep like I did?*

Then, as my husband and I walked our kids to the park, went for jogs around our riverside town, or left our neighborhood for custard, the flags started sprouting from the sides of the houses. One by one they grew, first one, then two, then three Confederate flags flown proudly from windows and flagpoles.

At the local library, I turned around from perusing the parenting section just long enough to see a man click on a video at one of the public computer stations. The video was of a woman talking directly into a camera with a Confederate flag flying behind her.

Fear.

There was a couple we'd seen a few times on walks and at our neighborhood park. They wore camouflage hats and jackets, and they never spoke a word to us. And that was after we'd spoken to them and our kids had played together.

More fear. Less sleep. Just paralysis.

I received notes of encouragement from the women with whom I'd traveled to Israel and Palestine, the same ones who'd demonstrated solidarity with me at the Shabbat meal.

Our church tried hard to find words of prayer and solace, words that condemned hate but didn't divide us.

In the midst of it all, fear was rising, suffocating me, making it hard for me to breathe and show up every day.

As I watched news and monitored social media with trepidation, I noticed one relationship that had already been strained was now more tense than ever: the relationship between the black community and members of the police force. In recent years, officers had been indicted or charged in the deaths of black individuals including Freddie Gray, Sandra Bland, Samuel DuBose, Philando Castile, and Terence Crutcher—yet only three convictions were served.[11]

Now, here we were, two sides warring with officers caught in the middle. Not only did I fear for my own life and the lives of my husband and kids, but I also now distrusted law enforcement more than ever before.

If I were in danger, would they protect and serve me?

Or would they see me as unimportant and disposable—a life that might have certain rights but that certainly doesn't matter?

I tried to think of all the honorable and brave men and women I knew who had served, both from my past and present—but somehow, their faces and names did little to allay the aftershock of hate.

The next day, I did the one thing I knew I could do.

You have to draw closer, I told myself. *Keep being fearful and holding people at arm's length, and it won't be the guns or the closet racists that kill you. It'll be your own paranoia and fear.*

I didn't know where to start. I asked myself whom I feared the most.

Cops, I admitted. I felt vulnerable and judged myself a little. But, to keep myself accountable, I texted my husband saying I wanted to have the cops over.

He was more than a little concerned. Being a black man who grew up on Chicago's South Side, he knew firsthand the ramifications of one innocent misstep in an interaction with the police.

But he gave me his support—and so I took action. I posted on Facebook,

> Open house: Dessert, coffee and (optional) prayer this afternoon at our home for any local law enforcement who want a space to voice how Charlottesville impacts them and how they "stand with" minority groups in their communities. We're with you, too. We want to understand. Proximity, dialogue and perspective matter! Message me for address/time if interested.

I almost wet my pants while typing those words, but I kept going—posting a similar message to our police department's Facebook page.

Friends came over to sit with us and be with our kids as we waited.

I'd baked chocolate chip cookies with my daughter and brewed coffee, the whole time telling myself this would never work and I was oversimplifying a complex issue.

This won't fix anything, Ashlee, I thought to myself. *Why do you think ever-loving* treats *will fix anything?*

But it was too late. I'd already taken a risk. I'd taken the risk to hold space and have conversation with people I'd already admitted I feared. I'd taken the risk in expressing my intention to people who knew cops, loved cops, *were* cops. I was sure "real" racial reconciliation and justice advocates were probably rolling their eyes at my sweet, sweet naiveté.

Who was I to think this would fix a single thing?

Midthought, a knock came at the door.

Two on-duty officers who'd parked their car down the street from our house actually showed up to talk to us. My husband and I answered as our friends sat on the couch, silent as church mice—making sure we could concentrate and they could hear.

We went outside to our porch, closing the door behind us. With a shaky voice, I spoke: "Officers, I—I mean, I know it's been a hard week . . . um, in our country. And, um . . ."

I stammered on and on, forgetting words and feeling foolish but somehow expressing our sorrow for what had transpired and our desire to know more about how events like Charlottesville affected their roles and responsibilities. We talked a little about community relations, and they made it clear, in few words, that they realized we were one of very few black families in the neighborhood. They talked about how quiet our community was and how they hadn't really needed to intervene in any major ways, which, admittedly, made my heart sink.

But the flags! I wanted to protest.

Then my daughter walked out with a tray of cookies.

The conversation shifted from rallies and protests to baseball and our upbringings. It wasn't long, but in looking these officers in the eye, in imperfectly expressing my truth and my concern—in offering a rickety olive branch in the form of confections and coffee—I couldn't fear them. I turned around and went back into my house.

Perhaps it was still true that I feared racists and unchecked power. I still cringed every time we passed by the Confederate flag waving wildly in a neighbor's yard. But I no longer feared those two police officers who knocked on my door and ate the cookies we'd baked. I couldn't fear them, because I'd met the fear with risk. As simple as it sounds, the risk was worth it. Even if just for that reason alone.

Shortly after the visit, the police department sent my kids police stickers—and then that Christmas we exchanged Christmas greetings through the mail.

We didn't see those officers again, but I knew they were around, somewhere. And I knew that just as we'd shared space with them, they'd shared space with us.

These days, taking a risk to step closer and share space can seem so small and insignificant: not grand or creative enough, not loud or witty enough. Risk can be a bold statement. Or it can be a quiet and bumbling peace offering, something we stumble and trip and stagger our way through, just trying to take a half step toward courage and harmony.

In this way, when it gets us closer to humanity and the stories that humanity tells, risk, no matter how small, is the greatest display of defiance.

Rather than stay comfortable behind our computer screens and newspapers, risk pulls us into the open, vulnerable and unsure, and helps us combat our fears with real human flesh.

Whom do you fear? What's her story?

Whom do you distrust? What's his greatest pride and joy?

Perhaps the cookies and coffee that day were pointless. Maybe they didn't make a difference at all.

But I slept just a little better that night.

We still ended up moving to a different neighborhood, partially because we felt unsafe. And we still have injustices to expose and mourn, not the least of which is how to explain systemic racism to my black son and daughters. I still cry when I hear breaking news of another black life lost. I still bite my tongue when white privilege flies freely around the room in cafés and conference rooms.

But the point is, the risk was for *that* day. For that day—just that day—the small risk was enough. We can be tempted into thinking that divisions and dissention require large and sweeping offerings of our well-crafted and clever selves. But what if we're too tired for clever? What if we're too ignorant for ingenious? What if all we have is a weary heart and a lot of fear? What if we've had enough and that means having nothing at all?

That Sunday afternoon the cookies and coffee were enough. Truly, they were all I had. And they were enough for me to grip tightly to hope in humanity and say *I think I can make it to tomorrow now, brave enough to find a way.*

And the thing about it was, I don't think I was the only one who took a risk that day. Two officers—two men who risk their lives every day—took a small but great risk too.

27

Chipotle

(Assumption)

I stood in line, dusty and dirtied from a morning filled with feed cups and fat sheep. My family and I had just spent the morning at a petting zoo by our house, and I'd underestimated the toll proximity to such friendly creatures would take on my wardrobe.

My black pants were covered in dirt from the sheep pen, and a rogue splotch of hand sanitizer had found its way to my right pant leg. Casper the llama had left nose snot on the sleeve of my white shirt in protest after I refused to give him even just one more handful of pellet feed. My black boots were filthy from walking around and around through loose mounds of dirt while my daughter squealed with delight as she rode Bubbles the pony.

On top of that, I'd untwisted my most recent hairstyle the night before and thrown it up into the messiest of crinkly Afro puffs that morning before rushing out of the house.

I was, to say the least, a sight to behold.

But we were hungry, and my husband was driving. So the task of running into Chipotle for our usual order of two kids' quesadilla meals, tacos, and a burrito bowl was left to me, the sheep whisperer.

I stood in line and crossed my arms instinctively, hoping the stench of farm-animal poo wasn't as obvious to others as it was to my own nose.

I approached the counter and ordered our food, not noticing the people around me until after I'd made my way past the black beans, brown rice, mild salsa, and sour cream, saying, "And may I please have a little side cup of cilantro? Yes, I know guacamole is extra."

As I was looking for my debit card to pay the cashier what seemed like my life's savings for a single helping of guacamole, a woman appeared next to me.

I glanced over and noticed that her face was kind and she was smiling. Her light brown hair just grazed the tops of her shoulders, and she had light green eyes and a disarming, easy gaze. I'd assumed she was coming to the counter for a to-go container for her burrito or some extra tortillas, but as I kept rummaging through my purse, I noticed she was waiting for me.

I stopped and looked her directly in the eye. It was then that I noticed her earrings. From each lobe dangled a leather cutout of Africa, large enough to reach almost the same place where her hair stopped.

I was instantly on guard. A pit formed in my stomach, and I knew it wasn't from the hunger pangs.

"Hi," I said, shortly.

"Oh hi," she said, sweetness dripping from her tongue as she drew out the *i*.

"You know," she continued, looking expectant, "I was sitting over there, and I saw you walk in . . . and I just want to say . . ."

I looked down and saw that she was clutching a wallet.

Oh no.

"Well, I'd just love to buy your meal and take some of the burden off you," she said. Her eyebrows were raised as high as they could go on her face.

I could tell she was excited. She was so proud of herself.

I was steaming mad, angry at how patronizing she seemed. She was speaking to me as if I were a child, someone who just *needed* her help.

I looked back to my purse, finally finding my debit card.

"You know, I got it," I said flatly, handing my card to the cashier.

He looked stunned, looking from me back to the woman, either struck by her audacity or wondering if maybe, perhaps, I actually were homeless.

"Are you sure?" she asked one more time, opening her wallet.

"Absolutely," I said.

I took the bag from the counter and rushed past her, all but running outside to the car. I got into our SUV and slammed the door shut, bursting into tears.

My husband looked up from his phone, eyes wide. "What happened in there?" he asked.

I told him, and through silent tears I mourned—once again—the pain that has punctuated my everyday moments for decades.

I was just dirty from a doggone farm.

But to her, I was dirty because I was inferior. My grimy presentation was enough to solicit her sympathy. And, therefore, I needed help. Her help. This was privilege at work.

But as I wiped the tears away with my dirty sleeve, I wondered how many times I'd been that woman—how many times I'd reached out with a full heart, eager to help, without knowing the least bit about a person's actual experience, moved only by her external appearance.

The assumptions we make, even with the best intentions, have the power to inflict the harshest wounds, forming craters where there could've been a bridge.

The conversation could've been so different if she had asked how my day was going, giving me a chance to tell her about my kids. We maybe could've talked about her earrings and why she felt so connected to Africa.

But because of one assumption, what she may have felt was kindness became cutting, and innocent care became an insult.

As my husband drove out of the parking lot, creating distance between her and me, I reflected on what was most important to me in the moments when I had to defend my dignity while digging out my debit card. As I grabbed the paper bag, walked inside our house, and set its contents on the kitchen table—a feast for my family that we paid for with our own hard-earned money—I decided that the kindness we show one another isn't more important than our stories.

Maybe the people to whom we choose to extend ourselves—whether homeless, in foster care, or ordering food in the chain restaurant—would like our help, but maybe they wouldn't.

Maybe instead of offering our charity, we should pull up a chair and simply listen to how they got their scars or their scuffs or their Africa earrings. Perhaps they'd prefer we stand back and let them go on their way, with a clear path to their next destination—saving the conversation for a better time, or not at all.

Our assumptions make false demands of people we hardly even know. We demand they receive from us, show us gratitude, say we're right. All without ever hearing them tell us of the places they've been and how they got there.

As I took a bite of my burrito bowl and wiped the guacamole from the crevice of my lip, I wondered how many people I'd deprived of dignity because of my big heart and faulty internal narratives. I wondered how many people on the street or in the restaurant or in my very own family weren't in need of help. Perhaps they were simply caught in the wake of one of life's dusty adventures, just trying to get home to eat.

The Cross I Bear

(Release)

Reclaiming human worth and embracing radical kindness will always require that we sacrifice something: our energy, our time, or our pride.

One of my favorite Scripture passages talks about what will be required of us if we choose to pursue sacrificial living the way Jesus did:

Don't push your way to the front; don't sweet-talk your way to the top. Put yourself aside, and help others get ahead. Don't be obsessed with getting your own advantage. Forget yourselves long enough to lend a helping hand.

Think of yourselves the way Christ Jesus thought of himself. He had equal status with God but didn't think so much of himself that he had to cling to the advantages of that status no matter what. Not at all. When the time came, he set aside the privileges of deity and took on the status of a slave, became *human*! Having become human, he stayed human. It was an incredibly humbling process. (Philippians 2:3–6, MSG)

Forget yourselves. What if the key to being brave and defying the divides that have formed in our families, our neighborhoods, our churches, and our friend groups has something to do with forgetting ourselves? What if the heaps of our demolished pride form the foundation for unity? What if we hold our stories with confidence and tenderness, appreciating what we've learned, but don't consider them or our values the most important thing?

This is the journey of humankindness: knowing and loving ourselves fully and honoring the hand life has dealt us, emptying ourselves for others, seeing the fullness of joy and hurt and pain in every interaction, and then choosing to regard another with humility and selflessness anyway.

I have a long way to go to live a life that reflects Paul's charge in Philippians 2, to extend kindness as he challenged in Ephesians 4: "Be kind and compassionate to one another, forgiving each other, just as in Christ God forgave you" (verse 32, NIV). But the unity of our humanity—achieved not by our own striving but because of a good God's perfect love and kindness toward us—is worth the continued pursuit.

This will require some flipped and tipped thinking, some stretched perspective. This will require some stillness and pause, some humiliation and sacrifice.

But at the end of the day, you must ask yourself, *Is our human unity worth my sacrifice?* I'm not talking about unity that is tolerant or fake, ignoring conviction and diluting identity. Mere tolerance and ignorance aren't kind. I'm talking about unity that rallies us together around our *imago Dei* and calls us to pursue relational healing with a higher purpose, anchored by the freeing power of the good news of grace.

Our one and only lives are meant to be lived in fullness—a fullness that honors our stories *and* the stories of strangers and neighbors and loved ones.

We can find our way back to one another. However, it will require all of us. After all, in the beginning what was true of and united our humanness was that God considered it *very good*.

At a church service a while back, I was standing in the front row next to the man who married my husband and me. He and his wife had recently journeyed a tough and largely public road in their marriage, but here we were, standing side by side in worship at the foot of the cross that towered above us onstage.

I'd had a particularly tough day and was finding it hard to focus. The burden was wearing on me, a black woman in a predominantly culturally white church who needed to show up with strength. I was weak. I was especially tired that day.

But in the middle of the worship service, this man leaned over to me and said, "Ashlee, I know that most of these people will never understand the cross you've had to bear. But I see you—and God sees you. And he loves you."

This man, this white man with a thick South African accent, summed up what humankindness means to me.

We all have burdens we've had to shoulder in life—circumstances that were hard to carry, that we never thought we'd live through. Some will never understand us, no matter how hard we try to tell our stories or justify our positions.

But if we're willing to release some of ourselves for the sake of another in the spirit of radical kindness, to let go of power, control, or other lesser gods that we've been gripping so tightly, with enough attention, care, and love, we can still acknowledge the complexity and sacredness of one another's lives, even if we never understand the whole story.

We can choose to see one another, to invite proximity and share space. We can listen and learn. We can remind one another that even when we get it wrong, we can continue to submit ourselves to the "incredibly humbling process" that Jesus himself endured. We can take heart in knowing that God sees us, and because of *his* loving-kindness toward us, we are able to grip tightly to a worth and identity defined in him, loving one another in ways beyond our own human strength and ability. And that loving, radical kindness, if we choose to accept and pursue it, will be what binds us, beautiful and imperfect, together again and again and again.

Questions for Personal Reflection or Group Discussion

Use this guide to reflect upon your own life—your own collection of stories and experiences. It may be used as an individual reflection exercise or to facilitate group discussion with friends, family, or coworkers. As you explore how life has shaped you and how your experiences have encouraged or discouraged humankindness, consider its power to elevate the worthiness and intrinsic value of your own story, as well as that of others around you. Each chapter in the book is accompanied by a theme that captures a gateway to humankindness. Use these themes to help direct your reflections and discussions. You can write your answers in the space that follows or reflect on these questions in a separate journal or notebook.

Curiosity	Acceptance	Commitment
Sacrifice	Proximity	Understanding
Honor	Perspective	Loss
Safety	Service	Silence
Humility	Audacity	Context
Adventure	Humiliation	Risk
Respect	Friendship	Assumption
Choice	Gratitude	Release
Belonging	Invitation	
Expectation	Rejection	

1. How has your own life experience enhanced or hindered your ability to see worth in others?

2. As you reflect on the chapter themes in the book, which have influenced your life significantly? What did each one teach you about yourself?

3. What events or circumstances in your life have been hardest to process? What positive circumstances have marked you?

4. Which themes seem less dominant in your story?

5. If those themes were dominant in someone else's life, how would you seek to understand better?

6. Which themes have most influenced the way you view other people's value, worthiness, and significance?

7. Which themes seem less prominent when you think about the ways you form relationships and interact with others?

8. List some people you know personally or have observed from afar whose worthiness is hard for you to elevate, value, and respect.

9. Keeping this list in mind, reread Philippians 2:3–6. What word or phrase sticks out the most? What next step would you like to take that would reflect that word or phrase?

10. How do you want to reinforce or integrate radical kindness in your life in order to elevate another person's worthiness, regardless of the circumstance?

11. Whom will you ask to hold you accountable to see the last step through?

Acknowledgments

"My thanksgiving is perpetual." These words, written by author and poet Henry David Thoreau, hang above my bed. They're a daily reminder of what I know to be true: no matter what the circumstances dictate within any given day, one can always find a good reason to extend gratitude over and over again. This book is the epitome of that belief.

For the pages you're holding now, perpetual thanksgiving is in order.

First, thank *you,* my readers. I truly believed that few would see kindness as worthy of engaging at this time and place in our history. But you're taking the challenge to find another way to unity and wholeness. We're in this together!

Thank you to my incredibly patient, kind, and talented agent, Alexander Field, of the Bindery. I remember exactly where I was sitting in Cook Street Coffee when you asked me what I wanted to write about. And then you listened. And now here we are. You're the definition of a champion, and I'm grateful to you. This was fun! Let's do it again, shall we?

To Ingrid Beck, my lovely editor, thank you for rising to the charge I gave you not just to make this a better book but to help make me a better writer. Many em dashes were saved in the process of birthing this project because of you.

Thanks to team WaterBrook: Andrew Stoddard, Kim Von Fange, Kathy Mosier, Laura Barker, Jamie Lapeyrolerie, and Brett Benson for caring about this message as much as I do and for working so hard to help it come to life and be launched into the world.

If you didn't know, it takes a village to console a writer who's trying to write a book . . . or something like that. Thank you to my village: Kylee

Pantanella, Jenny Potter, Rhianna Godfrey Johnson, and Bridgette for listening to every thought, idea, and unformed hope along the way—and for always telling me the truth in kindness; the Palatine Starbucks crew for making sure the back corner table was available for 5:00 a.m. head-to-heads with my manuscript; to my CrossFit families (hi, Easy!) for giving me a protected space to exhale and get stronger; Jan Troeger and Dawn Haecker for offering your homes to me as quieter safe havens away from my own beloved toddler-filled one; Austin Channing Brown and Jo Saxton for answering my silly questions and reminding me that I could actually do this while leaning into the fullness of my beautiful blackness; Danielle Strickland for writing the foreword of my dreams and for inspiring courage, unity, and kindness among women everywhere who are rising to challenges and platforms around them; Hannah Gronowski, Autumn Katz, and the Women Speakers Collective family for reminding me that this is good, holy work; Megan Tamte and the Evereve family for bringing so much *joy* to this process . . . and my closet; Scott Arbeiter, Eugene Cho, and our Rwanda crew for lighting a fire that I hope never dies out; Steve Carter for waiting patiently for me to realize that I had within me what you'd always known was there—and for sending the email that started this whole thing; Shauna Niequist for coaching me and using your voice to elevate mine so many times; and the Perry family for your unending love for me.

Thank you to every friend who said yes to his or her story being included here. You know who you are. My life is better because you're in it. And to the women of Duchesne Academy of the Sacred Heart, the amazing humans of USC's Somerville, the 2017 Telos trip, the Houston Sonics track club, and Jack and Jill of America Inc.: thank you for extending your kindness to me. It's marked me in indescribably valuable ways.

My three church families have raised me up and wrapped their arms around me, extending the loving-kindness of God the Father to me and my family in ways I'll never forget. To the communities of Willow Creek Community Church (especially the Midweek community), Mars Hill Bible Church, and First Metropolitan Church, thank you for letting me serve you and be a part of your body. Together, we are the broken and beautifully redeemed bride of Christ. I'm honored to have seen his hand at work in and through you. (To our amazing neighbors, the Mars Hill staff and Formation School family, GR wouldn't be home without you! To AJ and Elaina Sherrill, Troy and Lis Hatfield, Tim and Allie Nelson, Ashanti and Rahni Bryant, Belinda and Stephan Bauman, and Gary and Carol Burge, thank you for welcoming us like family!)

To my kids: I cannot type these words without feeling my heart flutter inside my chest because I *really* believe you're God's greatest gifts to me. My cup truly runneth over. To Brooklyn, my strong, sweet firstborn, thank you for leading us in the way of kindness; to Myles, my tender, lionhearted boy, thank you for showing us what fearlessness and faith look like; to Journey, our littlest love, thank you for gifting joy and peace to the places around you with your sweet smile and spirit. To Mom and Dad, for always believing in me and clearing the way for me to fly; to Sidney Jr., Amanda, Adrianne, and David for loving me so well as your little sister. To Mom Ruth, Donna, Brian, Nikki, and my Chicago family, thanks for opening your hearts and making space for me.

Finally, to my Delwin. Thank you for giving so much of yourself in order to create space for this passion of mine. For getting me out of the house at the crack of dawn, envisioning our kids for Mama's dreams, and praying the prayer you've prayed since our wedding day. He's answering it, and I'm the luckiest to be yours.

Notes

1. Spiros Zodhiates, Warren Baker, and George Hadjiantoniou, eds., *The Complete Word Study Dictionary: New Testament* (Chattanooga, TN: AMG, 1992), 1482.

2. Tim Ellis, "Alaska Highway 75th Anniversary: A Tribute to Veterans Who Helped Build 'Road to Civil Rights,'" KTOO Alaska Public Media, June 1, 2017, www.ktoo.org/2017/06/01/alaska-highway-75th-anniversary-tribute-veterans-helped-build-road-civil-rights.

3. Andrew Dansby, "By Slowing Things Down, DJ Screw Found Fame Fast," *Houston Chronicle,* October 6, 2016, www.chron.com/local/history/innovators-inventions/article/By-slowing-things-down-DJ-Screw-found-fame-fast-9827789.php.

4. Shawn Setaro, "Lil Keke Is More Self-Made Than Kylie Jenner (or You)," *Complex,* July 19, 2018, www.complex.com/music/2018/07/lil-keke-more-self-made-than-you.

5. Riding dirty, as defined by urbandictionary.com, means "driving a vehicle with any form of illegality," for example, expired plates, an expired license, possessing illegal drugs, and so on.

6. Dr. Maya Angelou, interview by Oprah, *Oprah's Master Class: The Podcast,* March 6, 2019, podcast, 5:45–6:15, https://art19.com/shows/master-class/episodes/c9181a72-2570-41ed-8770-caab4381e53b.

7. Marianne Rohrlich, "Feeling Isolated at the Top, Seeking Roots," *New York Times,* July 19, 1998, www.nytimes.com/1998/07/19/style/feeling-isolated-at-the-top-seeking-roots.html.

8. Ciara and Missy Elliott, "1, 2 Step," *Goodies,* BMG, 2004.

9. Gilberto Barrera, "Racism: An Ever Present Shadow," *Costa Rico News,* December 7, 2017, https://thecostaricanews.com/racism.

10. Maggie Astor, Christina Caron, and Daniel Victor, "A Guide to the Charlottesville Aftermath," *New York Times,* August 13, 2017, www.nytimes.com/2017/08/13/us/charlottesville-virginia-overview.html.

11. Jasmine C. Lee and Haeyoun Park, "15 Black Lives Ended in Confrontations with Police. 3 Officers Convicted," *New York Times,* October 5, 2018, www.nytimes.com/interactive/2017/05/17/us/black-deaths-police.html.